BEIJING
2008

BEIJING
2008

olympic memories

First published in 2008 by
A & C Black Publishers Ltd
38 Soho Square, London W1D 3HB
www.acblack.com

Copyright © PA Sport 2008
Edited by Peter Marshall, Mark Tattersall and Chris Wiltshire
Contributors: Simon Armstrong, Mark Bowering, Josh Burrows, Eleanor Crooks,
Richard Duncan, Steve Jones, Frank Malley, Matt McGeehan, Cordelia O'Neill,
Chris Phillips, Jon Phipps, Mark Staniforth, John Skilbeck, Matt Thomas,
Peter Whitfield, Martyn Ziegler

ISBN 978-1-408-11349-3

A CIP catalogue record for this book is available from the British Library.

Designed and typeset in Papyrus LET and Futura Book by PA Sport, Bridgegate,
Howden, East Yorkshire
Cover design by James Watson
Inside photography © PA Photos
Printed and bound in Spain by GraphyCems

This book is produced using paper that is made from wood grown in managed,
sustainable forests. It is natural, renewable and recyclable. The logging and
manufacturing processes conform to the environmental regulations of the country
of origin.

The Bird's Nest national stadium was a triumph of architectural engineering and the lighting of the Olympic flame was stunning.

But in decades to come, when we reflect on the 2008 Olympic Games, we will also remember the smiling faces, the meticulous organisation and the willingness of Beijing to draw back the curtains just a shade to allow the world to take a look at one of its most secretive nations.

We saw marathon runners pounding around Tiananmen Square, past the portrait of Chairman Mao, where in 1989 a lone student tried to halt a tank in one of the century's most iconic images. We watched cyclists pedalling along the Great Wall against a backdrop of tradition and antiquity. And we witnessed the most treasured memory of the 29th Olympiad of the modern era, a 6ft 5in athlete from Jamaica called Usain Bolt, who assumed the stance of an archer, slapped his head curiously and pushed back the frontiers of sprinting.

In 100 years' time, they will still talk about the way Bolt destroyed competitors in the 100m and 200m in world-record times. They will talk about him as they still do about Jesse Owens, who smashed Adolf Hitler's notion of Aryan supremacy at the 1936 Olympic

Games in Berlin. Bolt may have been the heartbeat of the Beijing Games, a man who brought an audible gasp whenever he ran, but there were many other highlights.

American swimmer Michael Phelps, who won eight gold medals in the Water Cube pool to add to his six in Athens, becoming the most successful Olympian of all time. Great deeds, dramatic stories, euphoria, pain – these

are what shape Olympic Games, and the hush that descended when China's 110m hurdling icon Liu Xiang limped out injured before the start of his race is also seared into the mind.

So is the sight of the Union Jack being hoisted up flagpoles all over China. What great expectation that brings for London in four years' time.

There were 47 medals collected in total by Team GB, 19 of them gold, and the

Faces of China past and present in Tiananmen Square

Olympic spirit of courage and determination was present in every one of them. It was a Games that saw Russia and Georgia competing in beach volleyball while their soldiers fired missiles at each other in much deadlier conflict.

It was a Games, too, in which America beat China in the battle of the superpowers – at basketball that is.

It was also a Games protected by line after line of soldiers from the People's Republic of China, ringing the Olympic park, standing straight – a reminder of the danger that threatens all major events these days.

The feared terrorism never materialised. The Beijing smog just about dissipated. The army of volunteers could not have been more helpful, and many observers declared the 29th Olympiad of the modern era the most enchanting Olympic Games the world has seen. ■

'For a long time, China has dreamed of opening its doors and inviting the world's athletes to Beijing for the Olympic Games. Tonight that dream comes true. Beijing, you are a host to the present and a gateway to the future.'
Jacques Rogge, President of the IOC

'The Olympic Movement is a valuable spiritual and cultural asset offered to humanity by the people of ancient Greece.'
Chinese President Hu Jintao

'The ultimate boast is Olympic gold.'
Tennis superstar Venus Williams

'They made Kenyans forget tribe and party. They made Kenyans proud to be Kenyans; one nation united under one flag, singing one anthem, living one dream.'
Kenyan Sports Minister Kinuthia Murugu amid troubles at home

'The city is embracing the greatest show on earth. It's like watching your kids wake up, open the curtains and see the back garden covered in snow for the first time.'
Lord Coe, Chairman of the London Organising Committee for the 2012 Games

'I feel very lucky just to be here. I've been moved to see so many athletes, and China has done really well.'
Closing ceremony cheerleader and Beijing student Ying Ying, 20

'Male bees live for one moment, then they die. For us swimmers this moment comes only once every four years.'
Austrian swimmer Markus Rogan has a unique take on the Olympics

'Everybody seems just so happy to see us. We're beginning to understand now that the whole nation has been following it.'
Triple cycling gold medallist Chris Hoy realises Team GB's impact after touching down in the UK

'You have people who are exceptions. You have Einstein. You have Isaac Newton. You have Beethoven. You have Usain Bolt.'
Stephen Francis, coach of Jamaican sprinter Asafa Powell, reflects on the remarkable Usain Bolt following the sprinter's record-breaking exploits which made him one of the star performers of the 2008 Games

'These have been an absolutely fantastic Games and there's no doubt that in terms of performance and theatre the Chinese have set the bar pretty high. But I think with British ingenuity, wit and resourcefulness, we are going to produce a Games that is going to be, in our own sweet way, just as fantastic.'
London Mayor Boris Johnson promises to match Beijing's spectacular exploits

'Beijing has done something absolutely stupendous that everyone there will remember for the rest of their lives.'
British Olympics minister Tessa Jowell after seeing the opening ceremony

'Having this experience in China was amazing. The biggest thing is having something different from every other Olympics, which makes it even more exciting. I've never competed in London and I'm looking to really experience more of the city and its culture and be able to prepare myself to swim some fast times.'
Record-breaking swimmer Michael Phelps enjoys his China experience

'I think the highlight was getting my picture taken with the teams. They were so gracious and grateful and excited. It was just a very uplifting experience.'
US President George W Bush on meeting American competitors

'The Beijing Olympic Games is a testimony of the fact that the world has rested its trust upon China.'
Liu Qi, President of the Beijing Organising Committee, at the closing ceremony

'It's inspiring to see the level of organisation in China. I think it is the best organised Olympics, everybody says so, but as the focus moves today to 2012 then people will look at London, look at Britain afresh and they'll see that we're a tremendously diverse country. They'll see that we're totally focused on inspiring people through sports.'
Gordon Brown soaks up the atmosphere at the closing ceremony in Beijing and looks forward to London 2012

'As the Olympic Games in Beijing draw to a close, I have been particularly impressed by the British and Commonwealth athletes who have taken part in this memorable competition and who have contributed so much to the spirit of these remarkable Games in the various disciplines. As a nation, we now look forward to holding the Olympic Games in London in 2012.'
The Queen hails the achievement of British athletes and welcomes the Games to London

It began and ended in a blaze of fire and, by the time it was over, there could be no doubt the 2008 Olympic Games would be nothing if not spectacular.

From the cool of 2,008 Fou drummers, the culture of Confucius and the control of kung fu fighters, it was a stunning way to raise the curtain on Beijing's moment in the spotlight.

In a four-hour spectacle, trapeze artists hovered, dancers gambolled around a giant globe, and 29 footprints, in the form of firework explosions, were sent skywards to symbolise the path of the 29th Olympic Games of the modern era.

Athletes from all 204 countries marched proudly around the track, bristling with endeavour.

As the Olympic flame was set ablaze after a wire-suspended 200ft-high lap of the stadium roof by Chinese artistic gymnastic gold medallist Li Ning, the president of the People's Republic of China, Hu Jintao, announced: 'I declare open the Games of Beijing celebrating the 29th Olympiad of the modern era.'

And the world joined together in anticipation of the greatest sporting show on earth. ■

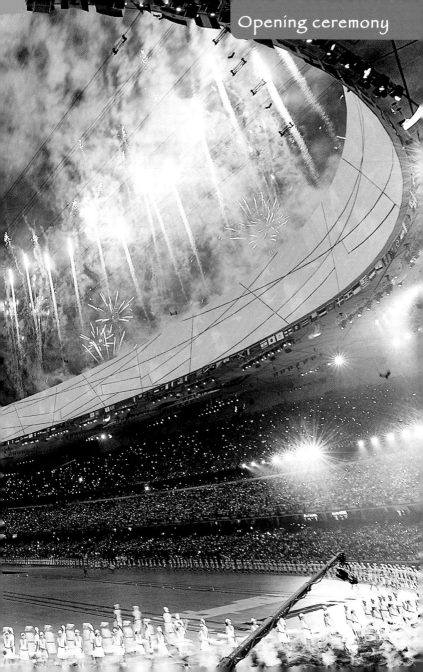

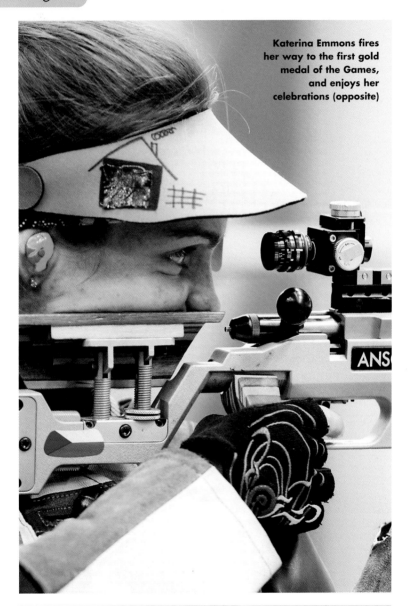

Katerina Emmons fires her way to the first gold medal of the Games, and enjoys her celebrations (opposite)

With the planning and the preparation over, competitors from 18 different sports finally got their Olympic challenge started on the opening day of action, and it was the name of Katerina Emmons that went down in the history books.

The 24-year-old from the Czech Republic had the honour of claiming the first gold medal of the Beijing Games as she won the women's 10m air rifle – equalling the world record in the process.

Emmons shot a perfect score in qualifying to tie the world's best mark and take a narrow one-point advantage over Russia's Lioubov Galkina, Croatia's Snjezana Pejcic and China's Du Li into the final.

Emmons then shot 103.5 for a final Olympic record total of 503.5 to claim a historic gold.

Afterwards she said: 'Thank God it's over, because I was so nervous. I had a headache this morning.

'I felt so terrible that I did not know how I would shoot, so to win the first gold medal of this Olympics is pretty amazing.

'I felt very nervous after the qualification round, the heart was beating fast. But I just told myself to concentrate on the final round. I cannot be more satisfied than this. I have

achieved the very best there is in sport. It's everything I could get.'

Home favourite and defending champion Du eventually finished out of the medals in fifth place. However, the host nation did not have too long to wait before they could celebrate. Weightlifter Chen Xiexia broke two Olympic records on the way to winning China's first gold medal of the Games as she easily won the women's 48kg competition.

She lifted an Olympic record 117kg in the clean and jerk, to go with the 95kg she had lifted earlier in the snatch, giving the 25-year-old an unassailable lead over her rivals.

Turkey's Sibel Ozkan took the silver medal and Chinese Taipei's Chen Wei-Ling claimed a bronze medal.

Shooter Pang Wei then doubled the Chinese tally when he kept his nerve to win the men's 10m air pistol competition. The 22-year-old beat South Korea's Jin Jong-oh into the silver medal position by just 3.7 points. North Korea's Kim Jong-su edged out United States' Jason Turner for the bronze medal with a strong finish.

The disparity between the very best athletes and the merely Olympic qualified was exposed in a brutal 248.5km men's cycling road race, which was won by Spain's Samuel

**Weightlifter Chen Xiexia
picks up China's first gold**

Spain's Samuel Sanchez is overcome at winning gold in the men's cycling road race

Sanchez. By the start of the final lap there was a maximum of 30 riders still in contention to claim victory, and by the last kilometre a lead group of just six riders had a chance of winning a medal.

A tough race of attrition proved too much for some of the 143 starters, 53 of whom dropped out during the seven laps of the hilly circuit.

Sanchez – who had finished seventh in the 2008 Tour de France – battled for position with Australian Michael Rodgers, Switzerland's Fabian Cancellara, Andy Schleck of Luxembourg, Alexandr Kolobnev of Russia and Italy's Davide Rebellin. And a well timed attack on the short, sharp rise to the finish earned Sanchez – the least fancied rider in a Spanish team featuring two past Tour de France winners and a triple world champion – the gold.

'I can't quite believe I've won the gold medal,' said the 30-year-old from Oviedo, whose biggest achievements prior to this had been his five stage victories on the Tour of Spain.

'My biggest fear was whether we'd be able to control the race as a team,

Mariel Zagunis (left) on her way to USA's first gold of the Games

and in such humid and tremendous heat. But we raced to perfection.'

South Korea's Choi Min-ho was a surprise winner of the men's -60kg judo as he defeated world number one Ludwig Paischer of Austria.

Romania's Alina Alexandra Dumitru claimed gold in the women's -48kg judo as an ippon saw her beat Cuban Yanet Bermoy.

In the same competition, Japanese defending champion Tani Ryoko defeated Lyudmila Bogdanova of Russia, also with an ippon, to claim the bronze. In doing so the 33-year-old joined an elite list of Olympians to win

medals at five consecutive Games, having claimed gold in Athens and Sydney, and silver in Atlanta and Barcelona.

China's early success was enough to put them at the top of the medal table at the end of the first day, but fellow Olympic heavyweights the United States were not far behind.

They opened their medal account on day one with a 1-2-3 in the women's fencing individual sabre as Mariel Zagunis defended her title with a 15–8 victory over teammate Sada Jacobson.

Rebecca Ward secured bronze by defeating Russian Sofiya Velikaya. ■

Romania's Alina Alexandra Dumitru claims gold in the -48kg judo

Nicole Cooke celebrates after her lung-bursting win in the women's cycling road race (right)

The rain poured and lightning lit up the skies over Beijing, but it was sunshine and smiles for Team GB as they celebrated their first success of the Games.

A superb ride from Nicole Cooke saw her win the women's cycling road race and get Britain off and running in the gold medal stakes.

The 25-year-old from the Vale of Glamorgan waited patiently for her chance in the 120km race, which took the peloton through the Badaling Pass and under the Great Wall of China twice.

She hit the front with 200m remaining and held on in a dramatic sprint finish to win ahead of Sweden's Emma Johansson and Tatiana Guderzo of Italy, who claimed the silver and bronze medals respectively.

It was just reward for the Welsh woman, who had been so disappointed to miss out on the medals with fifth place in Athens four years earlier.

'It was just joy at the end,' she said. 'There was just so much emotion coming out that I wasn't composed enough to give a proper salute, but I guess that's just the person I am.'

There was also reason to celebrate for former Olympic champion Jeannie Longo-Ciprelli of France. She was way down on Cooke in 24th place at the

Michael Phelps begins his epic Games with victory in the 400m individual medley

finish, but that still represented a remarkable achievement for the 50-year-old, competing in her seventh Games.

Over in the Water Cube, three world records were broken as the swimming programme sparked into life.

American star Michael Phelps underlined his determination to dominate the pool with the destruction of the world mark in the 400m individual medley as he picked up his first gold medal. Phelps was under world-record pace right from the start and eclipsed his own benchmark by an astonishing 1.41sec. Hungarian Laszlo Cseh touched in second place in a European-record time of 4min 6.16sec, while Ryan Lochte took third, almost two seconds further adrift, as Phelps crushed the field.

'That was a tough race the whole way through,' the American admitted. 'It wasn't comfortable in a close first 200m, but my breaststroke is stronger.'

Australian Stephanie Rice matched Phelps by destroying the world record in the women's 400m individual medley before the United States men's 4x100m freestyle relay team established another landmark time in their heats.

China claimed another four gold medals on day two as Xian Dongmei

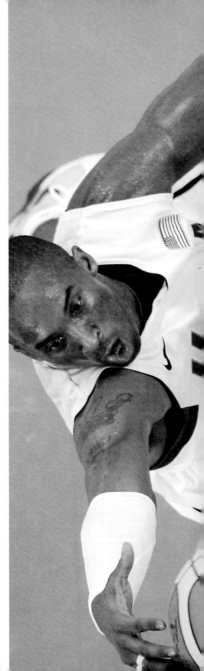

defended her Olympic crown in the women's -52kg judo, Guo Wenjun claimed the women's 10m air pistol crown, Guo Jingjing and Wu Minxia recorded their second consecutive Olympic success in the synchronised women's 3m springboard diving and 17-year-old Long Qingquan won the men's 56kg weightlifting.

But most of the attention in the host nation, and indeed around the world, was trained on the Beijing Olympic Basketball Gymnasium.

The United States and China – the superpower and the rising power – met on an Olympic basketball court, providing the hottest ticket in town, with an estimated television audience of one billion people watching around the world. The politicians were present, and American President George W Bush even got a cheer when he waved to the crowd, but sport was the main attraction.

The 7ft 6in NBA star Yao Ming – who had carried China's flag at the opening ceremony – led the hosts with 13 points and 10 rebounds, but they could not cope with the USA's strong defence and lightning-quick breakaways as the star-studded 'Redeem Team' won 101–70.

'We came out a little tight. We knew that it was going to be a very emotional game for both teams, especially China

Clash of the superstars as Kobe Bryant of the United States and China's Yao Ming go head to head on the basketball court

South Korea celebrate a sixth consecutive women's team archery gold medal

playing in front of their home crowd,' said US forward Chris Bosh. 'We withstood the storm, we calmed down, and we just played a lot better basketball.'

Meanwhile, outside, the rain could not prevent South Korea from dominating the women's team archery competition once again as they claimed their sixth consecutive gold medal.

Park Sung-hyun led them to victory as they set a 24-arrow world-record score of 231 in the quarter-final victory over Italy, and then went into the history books with a 224–215 win over China.

The fencing tournament was far less predictable. Athens gold medallist Jerome Jeannet of France had been expected to fight it out with reigning world champion Krisztian Kulcsar of Hungary for top honours, but when both were eliminated in the early stages the way opened up for Matteo Tagliariol to win individual épée gold for Italy for the first time in 40 years.

In the football tournament, Brazil captain and AC Milan star Ronaldinho scored twice as the *Seleção* gave New Zealand a footballing lesson in a 5–0 victory, while Argentina dominated their clash with Australia, but left it late to get the goal from Ezequiel Lavezzi which secured a 1–0 win and their passage into the quarter-finals. ∎

Ronaldinho gets off to a flying start with two goals for Brazil in their opening 5–0 win over New Zealand

Abhinav Bindra is congratulated on his gold medal by Indian IOC member Radhir Singh

Day three was a day of firsts as Olympic history was created on several fronts.

India had never won an individual Olympic gold medal in any sport prior to Beijing, although they had won team gold eight times in field hockey, with their last success coming at the Moscow Olympics in 1980. But all that changed when Abhinav Bindra shot his way to glory in the men's 10m air rifle competition.

The 25-year-old kept his composure in a nailbiting finale, producing a near-perfect 10.8 with his last shot to win gold.

In doing so, the former child prodigy completed a fairytale rise to the top of his sport, and became India's latest sporting icon.

Bindra – from an affluent family who had helped their son's career progress by installing an indoor range in their back yard – led the news broadcasts on Indian television channels and websites, and dignitaries back home were soon lining up to praise him.

Even the country's president, Pratibha Patil, lauded his feat, saying in a personal message to the marksman: 'I am extremely delighted and proud to hear that you have realised the dream of a billion of our people. Your achievement today should inspire

British swimmer
Rebecca Adlington
realises gold is
hers in the 400m
freestyle and
(inset above)
celebrates with
bronze medallist
Joanne Jackson

confidence amongst all Indian sportspersons that they can achieve the pinnacle of any sport at the international level.'

Bindra was a modest champion, saying: 'It's the thrill of my life. It's hard to describe.'

Those sentiments were soon being echoed at the Water Cube as Great Britain's Rebecca Adlington created her own piece of history.

The 19-year-old from Mansfield became the first Briton in 20 years to win a swimming gold medal with a stunning victory in the 400m freestyle.

Adlington claimed gold ahead of American pre-event favourite Katie Hoff in a thrilling fingertip finish, winning by just 0.07sec, while teammate Joanne Jackson took the bronze.

Adlington earned a hero's welcome back at the Olympic Village. She said: 'When I got back the team had stuck on the door "Congratulations Becky". Me and Jo walked into the team meeting and everyone stood up and gave us a massive round of applause.

'It's every sportsperson's dream. I'm going to hold on to the medal. I've had it on all afternoon and I don't want to take it off.'

Adlington's achievement even overshadowed the great Michael Phelps, who claimed his second gold medal of the Games in the men's 4x100m freestyle relay as he and his United States teammates beat France in world-record time.

There was also a world record for Kosuke Kitajima in the 100m breaststroke, the Japanese becoming the first man to break the 59-second barrier ahead of Norway's Alexander Oen and France's Hugues Duboscq.

Australia's Libby Trickett won the women's 100m butterfly final.

Teenage British star Tom Daley dived into elite Olympic company on day three in a story that fascinated the world. The 14-year-old caught the imagination of the international media in the build-up to the Games as he took a break from his school holidays to compete in Beijing.

Daley coped admirably with the hype to reach the final of the men's synchronised 10m platform with Blake Aldridge. The British duo could not

Tom Daley (right) and Blake Aldridge airborne in the final of the men's synchronised 10m platform diving

Zhang Xiangxiang kisses the weights after winning gold in the men's 62kg weightlifting

compete with China's reigning world champions and eventual winners Lin Yue and Huo Liang, but Daley still drew admiring glances from spectators and competitors alike.

'It was a great experience,' Daley said. 'I really enjoyed myself.'

There was more success for the hosts when China secured double gold in the weightlifting thanks to Zhang Xiangxiang in the men's 62kg competition and defending champion Chen Yanqing in the women's 58kg.

In the tennis, Roger Federer cruised into the second round with a 6–4 6–2 victory over Russia's Dmitry Tursunov. Wimbledon champion Rafael Nadal was not so comfortable but progressed all the same, needing three sets to see off Italian Potito Starace.

In the women's event, fourth seed Serena Williams won all but four games

to complete victory over Olga Govortsova in a match held over due to rain on Sunday.

South Korea continued to dominate the archery as their men's team set a 24-arrow Olympic record on their way to a two-point victory over Italy.

In the judo, world number one Elnur Mammadli needed just 13 seconds to defeat South Korea's Wang Ki-chun with an ippon to claim gold in the men's

-73kg class. Meanwhile, Italy's Giulia Quintavalle won gold in the women's -57kg category by beating Deborah Gravenstijn with a yuko, and Satu Makela-Nummela of Finland won gold in the women's trap.

And there was further drama in the fencing as Italy's Maria Valentina Vezzali beat South Korea's Nam Hyun-hee 6–5 in the women's individual foil final. ■

The superpowers came to the fore on a day dominated by China and America.

The United States' stranglehold over events in the pool continued at the Water Cube, with three more gold medals highlighting another run of star-spangled success.

That man Michael Phelps led the way with his third of the Games, setting a new world record in the men's 200m freestyle with a time of 1min 42.96sec, to win his ninth Olympic title.

And compatriots Aaron Peirsol and Natalie Coughlin soon joined him on the top step of the podium. Coughlin successfully defended the 100m backstroke title she had won in Athens with a superb performance to beat the hot favourite, Zimbabwean veteran Kirsty Coventry.

Coughlin led the race from the start and was the first to reach the turn with Coventry close behind. Coventry, who broke Coughlin's world record in the semi-finals earlier in the week, tried to catch up in the final 50m, but Coughlin held off the challenge.

Soon after, Peirsol smashed his own world record to win the 100m backstroke title, touching the wall ahead of teammate Matt Grevers in a time of 52.54sec, 0.35sec under the mark he had set at the US trials a month earlier.

Natalie Coughlin heads for gold in the
100m backstroke, while Michael Phelps
and Aaron Peirsol (below) made it three
golds on the day for the United States

'It doesn't get any easier, to be honest,' said the American as he reflected on his achievement. 'The knowledge and experience that you have done it once, and can probably do it again, does help. That is what I tried to keep in mind, but I really wanted to race and the guys around me pushed me to what I did today.

'I couldn't see those guys,' he added, having trailed before the turn. 'I just swam my own race. We [Phelps and Grevers] were just trying to go one-two the whole time.'

Australian world champion Leisel Jones did manage to break the United States' monopoly of the medals when she won the women's 100m breaststroke title by a comfortable margin. That was redemption for the swimmer from Katherine in the Northern Territory, who had suffered Olympic heartbreak twice previously.

Jones had narrowly missed out on gold in Sydney in 2000, and it was a similar story in Athens when she took silver in the 200m breaststroke and bronze in the 100m breaststroke, despite starting as the favourite to win both events.

After finally realising her dream she admitted: 'It has been a long journey. It has been a long eight years, and there was just a lot of relief that the training

Leisel Jones
finally takes gold
after eight years
of heartbreak,
and shows her
delight on the
podium (left)

Chen Yibing helps
China to gold in the
men's artistic
gymnastics team
final, while Zhong
Man (opposite)
wins the hosts' first
ever fencing gold

was definitely worth it. The Athens experience has made me a much stronger person and much stronger athlete.'

There were four more gold medals for China as the celebrations continued for the hosts. Teenage pair Wang Xin, 16, and Chen Ruolin, 15, won the host nation's third gold medal out of three in the diving competition as they claimed victory in the synchronised women's 10m platform.

They were followed by the men, who collected the first artistic gymnastics gold medal of the Games, ahead of silver medallists Japan and the United States, who took the bronze medal.

At the Beijing University of Aeronautics and Astronautics Gymnasium, 20-year-old Liao Hui lifted his way to victory in the men's 69kg weightlifting competition.

And further history was made when Zhong Man beat France's Nicolas Lopez 15–9 to win China's first-ever fencing gold.

Germany collected the opening equestrian medal of the Games when they won the three-day team eventing competition in Hong Kong, much to the delight of one of the successful riders, Hinrich Romeike. 'I feel happy, very

Day 4

happy. I'm thankful to possess such a wonderful horse,' Romeike said of his mount, Marius.

On the tricky course at the Shunyi Olympic Rowing-Canoeing Park, experienced paddler Michal Martikan of Slovakia turned back the clock as he recaptured the men's slalom canoe single title he had won 12 years previously in Atlanta in 1996.

The 29-year-old edged out Britain's David Florence, while defending champion Tony Estanguet of France failed in his bid for a third consecutive gold medal as he finished down in ninth place.

Germany's Alexander Grimm swept to victory in the men's slalom kayak single competition and then struggled to contain his emotions. He admitted: 'I have never had a feeling like that before at any competition. Everything fitted perfectly.'

In the shooting, South Korea's Jin Jong-oh took gold in the men's 50m pistol to add to the silver he won in the men's 10m pistol, while Walton Eller of the United States set a new Olympic qualifying record of 145 on his way to winning the men's double trap.

Germany's Ole Bischof threw South Korea's Kim Jae-bum for a yuko to claim victory in the men's -81kg judo with Japan's Tanimoto Ayumi needing just

1min 26sec to defend her title by beating France's Lucie Decosse with an ippon in the women's -63kg.

Elsewhere, Russia dominated the opening day of the Greco-Roman wrestling with Islam-Beka Albiev overpowering Azerbaijan's Vitaliy Rahimov in the final of the men's 60kg and Nazyr Mankiev taking the honours in the 55kg category. Pak Hyon-suk won

44

Britain's David Florence is pipped into the silver medal position in the slalom canoe by Michal Martikan of Slovakia (below)

North Korea's first gold medal of the Games in the women's 63kg weightlifting with a total lift of 241kg.

And in the team sports, the preliminary round of the men's water polo competition at the Yingdong Natatorium saw Croatia defeat 2008 World League champions Serbia to round off an action-packed day across a host of venues. ■

Nine world records fell on day five as Michael Phelps completed his quest to become the most successful Olympic athlete of all time.

With minutes to go before the American dived into the pool at the National Aquatics Centre to make history, he received two texts from a friend back in Baltimore.

The first read: 'It's ridiculous how many times a day I have to see your ugly face.'

The second was a little kinder, saying: 'It's time to be the best ever.'

An hour or so later he was just that, having increased his Olympic gold medal tally to 11, six in Athens in 2004 and five in Beijing.

The American claimed the 10th and 11th gold medals of his amazing career with typically dominant performances.

Phelps collected his fourth Beijing gold in the 200m butterfly, and made it five out of five just under an hour later as part of the United States' 4x200m freestyle relay team – with world records falling both times.

Following his heroics in Athens four years previously and his earlier efforts in Beijing, he surpassed the total of nine career golds won by Finnish runner Paavo Nurmi, American track and field star Carl Lewis, former Soviet gymnast Larysa Latynina and fellow US swimming legend Mark Spitz, to cement his place in Olympic history.

'I'm almost at a loss for words,' said Phelps. 'To be the most decorated Olympian of all time, it just sounds weird. I am speechless.

'It started to sink in a little after the butterfly. I was trying to focus on my next race but I kept thinking, "Wow. Greatest Olympian of all time". It's a pretty neat title, and I'm definitely honoured.

'When you have an Olympic gold medal it stays with you forever. It never gets old listening to your national anthem with a gold medal around your neck.'

And the achievement was made all the more remarkable when Phelps

Main image:
Michael Phelps
prepares for the
200m butterfly final

Inset below: Phelps
and teammates
celebrate victory in
the 4x200m
freestyle relay

revealed he was swimming 'blind' for much of the butterfly final, which he won in a stunning time of 1min 52.03sec.

'I couldn't see anything for the last 100m,' he said. 'My goggles pretty much filled up with water. It just kept getting worse and worse through the race, and I was having trouble seeing the walls to be honest. But it's fine. I wanted to break the record and wanted to go 1min 51sec or better, but in the circumstances I guess it's not too bad.'

As expected, Phelps was chosen to lead off the American quartet in the 4x200m relay, swimming the first leg more than two seconds under world-record pace.

His teammates, Ryan Lochte, Ricky Berens and Peter Vanderkaay, carried on where he had left off and eventually clocked a new world-record time of 6min 58.56sec – the first time the seven-minute barrier had been broken. The new record was almost five seconds quicker than the previous best.

World records were the order of the day as France's Alain Bernard and Australian Eamon Sullivan earlier traded times in the 100m freestyle.

Bernard clocked a time of 47.20sec in winning the first semi-final, beating the previous mark set by Sullivan in the 4x100m relay earlier in the week. But

Australian
Eamon
Sullivan and
Alain Bernard
of France (left)
traded world
records in the
100m
freestyle

Kristin Armstrong heads for victory in the women's individual time trial, while Fabian Cancellara (opposite) wins the men's equivalent

Sullivan then went even quicker in the second semi-final, recording a time of 47.05sec to reclaim the record and set up a mouth-watering final showdown.

Another world record was broken in the women's 200m freestyle, Italian Federica Pellegrini taking the gold medal in a time of one minute 54.82sec to lower her own mark.

Yet another world record went in the women's 200m individual medley, with Australian Stephanie Rice lowering her previous best by 0.47sec. Rice won gold, just ahead of Zimbabwe's Kirsty Coventry, with American Natalie Coughlin in third place.

On the road, Fabian Cancellara of Switzerland powered to victory in the men's cycling individual time trial as he lived up to his pre-race favourite status over the gruelling 47.3km course. The double world time trial champion held off a strong challenge from silver medallist Gustav Larsson of Sweden, while American Levi Leipheimer took the bronze medal.

'When I heard on the radio earpiece that I was six seconds back to Larsson I started giving it everything. I didn't want to lose today,' said Cancellara, who hit speeds of up to 80kph in the final few kilometres. 'I've been world champion twice, but this has been the focus for so long. I told myself that going home

without the gold is a failure. I've prepared specifically for this race and made a lot of sacrifices.'

Kristin Armstrong of the United States won the women's individual time trial ahead of early leader Emma Pooley of Great Britain. Pooley set the benchmark time and held on to it for a long period, but she was eventually edged out by the American by just over 24 seconds.

China completed a clean sweep of the synchronised diving competitions as Qin Kai and Feng Wang won the men's synchronised 3m springboard event.

That was followed by a first-ever gold medal for the hosts in the team event of the women's gymnastics, before Liu Chunhong broke three world records on her way to winning gold in the women's 69kg weightlifting competition.

Liu lifted 128kg in the snatch, 158kg in the clean and jerk and 286kg in total weight. And there was yet more home success when sharp-shooter Chen Ying emerged victorious in the women's 25m pistol final, while Steeve Guenot of France and Georgia's Manuchar

Georgia celebrate as Russia trudge off after a poignant beach volleyball encounter

Kvirkelia won gold in the Greco-Roman wrestling.

Meanwhile, South Korea's Sa Jaehyouk powered his way to gold in the men's 77kg weightlifting category, Germany claimed double fencing gold as reigning world champion Britta Heidemann defeated Romanian Ana Maria Branza in the final of the women's individual épée, and Benjamin Philip Kleibrink triumphed in the men's individual foil with a 15–9 win over Japan's Ota Yuki.

At Chaoyang Park, hours after their nations had declared an uneasy truce in the disputed border region of South Ossetia, Russia and Georgia fought a battle of a different kind on the beach volleyball court. Brazilian-born pair Christine Santanna and Andrezza Chagas took up the invitation of the Georgian president's wife, herself a keen beach volleyball player and fan, to represent their adopted country, and duly triumphed in a thrilling match, rallying from the brink of elimination to stay in the competition and send the Russians home. ■

The weather wreaked havoc in Beijing and beyond as thunderstorms forced the postponement of several outdoor sports.

The entire day's sailing programme at Qingdao, the finals of the men's slalom canoe doubles, the women's slalom kayak singles and most of the baseball action fell victim to the heavy rain, while play was also suspended in the tennis – although not before American James Blake had managed to cause an upset by defeating world number one Roger Federer in the quarter-finals.

The heavens also opened at the Beijing Olympic Green Archery Field, soaking the competitors. But even that was not enough to prevent Zhang Juanjuan of China breaking South Korea's 24-year hold on the women's individual archery competition as she claimed victory with the last arrow of a nail-biting final against Park Sung-hyun.

Park, the world number one, had started the contest as a heavy favourite but fell to a shock defeat when 27th seed Zhang produced a decisive last arrow to take the gold. Zhang had earlier beaten world number two Yun Ok-hee in an equally thrilling semi-final contest.

'I had a dream for the gold. I was on a mission,' Zhang told reporters. 'The

China's Zhang Juanjuan ends South Korea's 24-year domination of the women's individual archery

entire Chinese archery world breathed a sigh of relief. 'I think this is the result of the efforts of all the Chinese archers. It should also be attributed to the cheers and spectators, and to my confidence and composure. I've been thinking about this every day,' Zhang added. 'I was prepared for it, for the Koreans.'

Park wiped away the tears after the gold-medal match.

'I do regret the result,' she said. 'I am very sad in a way, because I feel I may have broken the tradition set by those archers who were before me. However, I feel that by winning the silver, it will make me crave the gold more, and make me appreciate the gold more in the future, so I think it's a good experience.'

On a day that saw the Asian nations enjoy plenty of success, Japan's Kosuke Kitajima underlined his status as the greatest breaststroke swimmer of all time by successfully defending both the titles he had won in Athens four years previously.

The 25-year-old claimed gold in the 200m breaststroke in an Olympic-record time to complete the double-double – the first time the feat

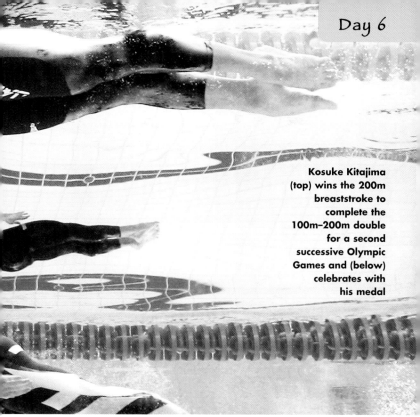

Kosuke Kitajima (top) wins the 200m breaststroke to complete the 100m–200m double for a second successive Olympic Games and (below) celebrates with his medal

Yang Wei wins more gold for China in the men's individual all-around gymnastics

Beijing was the end of the road for Pieter van den Hoogenband

has been achieved. Kitajima won the 100m title earlier in the week and, added to the two world titles he achieved in Barcelona in 2003 and the gold he won at the World Championships in the 200m in Melbourne in 2007, it was enough to set the Tokyo native apart from any other breaststroke swimmer in history.

Kitajima touched the wall in a time of 2min 07.64sec to finish just outside his own world record and ahead of second-placed Brenton Rickard of Australia.

China claimed their first gold medal in the pool as Liu Zige shattered Jessicah Schipper's world record in the 200m butterfly to finish ahead of compatriot Jiao Liuyang.

Pieter van den Hoogenband's bid to become the first male swimmer to win three consecutive Olympic titles came to an end when France's Alain Bernard stormed to victory in the final of the 100m freestyle. The tall 25-year-old beat world record holder Eamon Sullivan by just 0.11sec. Van den Hoogenband finished fifth and then announced his retirement.

'This is my last race,' the 30-year-old said. 'I've raced many times against Alain, but I didn't know he was in my league. We met before the races and he's a great guy and we have a good relationship. I'm very happy with an ambassador like Alain. He's a great sportsman.

'It's a new generation and it's now time to step aside,' Van den Hoogenband added. 'They did a great job. I'm from the previous generation.'

Australia won the women's 4x200m freestyle relay, destroying the world record by well over five seconds to hold off second-placed China and the United States.

Yang Wei took yet another gold for China in the men's individual all-around gymnastics, while compatriot Du Li added further success in the women's 50m rifle.

The Czech Republic's Katerina Emmons – who had claimed the first gold medal of the Games in the

Chiara Cainero of Italy wins the women's skeet after a shoot-off

women's 10m air rifle on day one – had to settle for silver this time.

Chiara Cainero of Italy held her nerve to win the women's skeet after being tied on 93 hits with the United States' Kimberly Rhode and Germany's Christine Brinker. That forced a shoot-off, but Brinker and Rhode missed their second shoot-off target, so gold went to Cainero, who successfully hit both of hers.

Tuvshinbayar Naidan threw Askhat Zhitkeyev of Kazakhstan for a waza-ari to give Mongolia their first-ever Olympic gold medal in the men's -100kg judo, and China's Yang Xiuli took the honours in the women's -78kg competition by defeating Yalennis Castillo of Cuba with a hantei.

Ukraine won the gold in the inaugural women's team sabre, beating China 45–44.

Italy's Andrea Minguzzi overcame Hungary's Zoltan Fodor to take the men's Greco-Roman 84kg wrestling title, while Aslanbek Khushtov of Russia earned the honours in the 96kg category with Mijain Lopez of Cuba taking 120kg gold.

In the men's basketball competition, the United States continued to sweep all before them with a third straight victory, 92–69 over Greece, taking them to the top of their group.

Twins Peter and Pavol Hochschorner take gold for Slovakia in the C2 canoe slalom, while (inset above) shooter Matthew Emmons is congratulated by wife and fellow medallist Katerina

There was double joy in the Hochschorner household as the Olympic Games entered their second week, but twins Peter and Pavol were not the only ones keeping it in the family.

The Slovakian siblings made history by winning an unprecedented third canoeing slalom Olympic gold, extending their long period of dominance in the men's C2 event. They won comfortably with a combined time of 190.82sec, despite a penalty of four seconds for hitting two gates in the semi-final and final runs.

Ondrej Stepanek and Jaroslav Volf of the Czech Republic improved one place on their Athens finish to take the silver medal, while Mikhail Kuznetsov and Dmitry Larionov of Russia took bronze. However, there was no doubting who deserved the headlines.

'It's one boat and a pair of people, so it doesn't matter as much that we're brothers,' said Peter as he reflected on another gold to add to their triumphs in

Athens and Sydney. 'It always has to be a team to co-operate, and to be friends. We will keep competing for as long as we can.'

Elsewhere, there were more memories for the family album for the United States' Matthew Emmons, who followed up his Czech wife Katerina's achievements in winning shooting gold and silver earlier in the Games with a medal of his own.

He took silver in the men's 50m rifle prone, behind Artur Ayvazian of the Ukraine. But it was to be a bittersweet week for the American, who would later produce a woeful final shot in the men's 50m rifle three positions to drop from first to fourth and blow his chances of gold. For now, though, he was celebrating. 'This is the best match of my life. It is the best I can shoot,' he said. 'I had to fight harder than ever. The wind just swirled around. It was definitely challenging, but those kinds of conditions really show off the best.' Talking about his champion wife, who

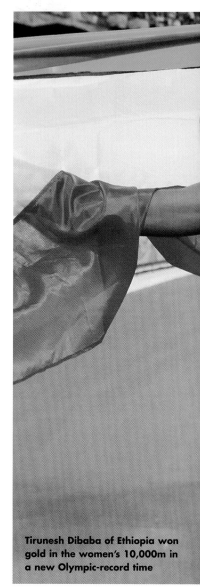

shot for her native Czech Republic, Emmons added: 'Her success gives me good energy and great motivation. I want to do well, too. She congratulated me after the final. She knew it was the best I can shoot.'

On the opening night of the track and field programme, there was no shortage of drama inside the Bird's Nest.

Tirunesh Dibaba of Ethiopia won gold and set a new Olympic record in the women's 10,000m, while the opening rounds of the men's 100m saw all the big names ease through.

Hyleas Fountain of the United States held the lead in the heptathlon after four of the seven disciplines, while Rashid Ramzi of Bahrain clocked the fastest time in the opening heats of the men's 1500m.

Maria Mutola of Mozambique was the fastest of 24 qualifiers in the women's 800m, while Tomasz Majewski won gold in the men's shot put final.

In the pool, Michael Phelps took his sixth gold medal as he destroyed the opposition once again to win the 200m individual medley. He set yet another world record with a time of 1min 54.23sec as he destroyed a field that was expected to provide him with one of his more serious challenges.

Rebecca Soni added another gold medal for the Americans as she

Tirunesh Dibaba of Ethiopia won gold in the women's 10,000m in a new Olympic-record time

Britta Steffen of Germany recovers after winning the 100m freestyle, while Ryan Lochte (opposite) is jubilant at winning the 200m backstroke

powered past Leisel Jones in the final 75m to win the 200m breaststroke in a new world-record time.

Earlier, Ryan Lochte had claimed gold in the 200m backstroke ahead of Aaron Peirsol, while Russian Arkady Vyatchanin took bronze and Germany's Britta Steffen won the 100m freestyle, touching just ahead of world-record holder Libby Trickett.

The 24-year-old's gold medal was all the more surprising given that she was in last position at the halfway mark. Yet she came from behind to clock the third-fastest time in history.

'It's an amazing feeling, and I never thought that I would make this final breakthrough,' said Steffen. 'I am now

an Olympic champion and that is amazing.'

Trickett, meanwhile, was not too upset with her silver medal. She was just thankful to be swimming in the final at all after a slow time in the heats meant she had to rely on the disqualification of Chinese swimmer Pang Jiaying.

'I was ninth after the semi-finals. I was out of the final, so to get put in and come away with a silver is awesome,' she said.

The United States claimed a one-two in the women's individual artistic gymnastics all-around competition as Nastia Liukin took gold ahead of Shawn Johnson, while Ukraine's Viktor Ruban scored a narrow 113–112 victory over

Park Kyung-mo of South Korea in the men's individual archery final.

There was a shock for defending champion Tsukada Maki of Japan on the final day of the judo action as she was thrown for an ippon by gold medallist Tong Wen of China in the women's +78kg category.

Japanese spirits were lifted when Ishii Satoshi claimed gold in the men's +100kg event by defeating Abdullo Tangriev from Uzbekistan with a yuko.

China's superb weightlifting record was extended when Lu Yong edged past Andrei Rybakou of Belarus in the men's 85kg category by virtue of a lighter body weight after both men lifted a total of 394kg. And Cao Lei added more home success with an Olympic record to win the women's 75kg event.

There was a perfect start to the track cycling for Great Britain when Chris Hoy, Jamie Staff and Jason Kenny won gold in the team sprint.

Britain hit the finishing line in a time of 43.128sec, more than half a second faster than the French. In doing so, they delivered a statement of intent for the five days of racing ahead – and a sign of things to come. ◾

**Great Britain
clinch gold in
the team sprint**

Usain Bolt laps up the adulation after his astonishing win in the 100m final (right)

It had been billed as the defining day of Beijing 2008 and 'Super Saturday' lived up to every bit of the hype as Usain Bolt provided the iconic image of the Games with a stunning victory in the 100m final in world-record time.

The scoreboard in the Bird's Nest stadium flashed the words 'Amazing' and 'Fantastic', and repeated them in Chinese. But in truth, no language has any adjectives that come close to doing justice to the manner in which the Jamaican announced himself as the new Olympic champion, the fastest man on the planet and the most exciting athlete in the world. The 100m showpiece had been built up as the race of the century: a duel between Bolt and Asafa Powell. In fact, it was nothing of the sort. It was hardly a race at all.

It was a procession behind 21-year-old Bolt, who led the others home like a showboating baton-twirler at the head of the parade.

The time clocked was 9.69sec, which lowered Bolt's own world record by three hundredths of a second. Richard Thompson of Trinidad and Tobago trailed two tenths of a second behind – a huge distance in 100m terms – while

Walter Dix of the USA finished in third place.

The Jamaican was so much in control of the race that he found the time to celebrate before crossing the line in front of a packed crowd. Bolt admitted afterwards it could have been even faster, saying: 'I'm just happy. I came here to prove that I'm the best in the world, and I did that. I came here with a plan and I executed it.

'I don't really know what happened. I even could be 9.60. As soon as I saw I had covered the field and I knew I would win, I was very happy and I

started to celebrate. I wasn't worried about the time. I just came here to win.'

Bolt's breathtaking run even overshadowed the achievements of Michael Phelps, who equalled Mark Spitz's record haul of seven gold medals at a single Games with victory in the Water Cube in the most dramatic fashion in the 100m butterfly.

Phelps trailed Serbian swimmer Milorad Cavic for almost the whole race but somehow managed to touch just 0.01sec in front to draw level with Spitz's landmark, set in Munich in 1972. The pool also provided the

Michael Phelps equalled Mark Spitz's record haul of seven golds in a single Games by winning the 100m butterfly, while Britain's Rebecca Adlington (below) won her second, the 800m freestyle

setting for the start of a golden day for Great Britain when Rebecca Adlington claimed the first of nine medals, including four golds, in the 800m freestyle.

It represented the country's best day in the Olympics for 100 years, with Britain also on the top step of the podium at the Shunyi Olympic Rowing Park and the Laoshan Velodrome.

Teenager Adlington, who had claimed a last-gasp victory in the 400m, ensured the result was in no doubt in her favourite event as she led from the start before touching the wall in a time

The derny leads the riders
round the track in the
early stages of the keirin

of 8min 14.10sec, smashing a 19-year-old world record in the process. Teammate Cassie Patten, who finished eighth, hugged Adlington afterwards and turned to the television cameras to announce: 'If the Queen is listening to this: two golds – Dame Rebecca Adlington!'

Adlington was shocked by the record, saying: 'I can't believe it. It hasn't sunk in yet. Obviously I knew I had won gold but I didn't expect that time at all.'

Zimbabwe's Kirsty Coventry finally claimed gold after three silvers, winning the 200m backstroke in a world-record time of 2min 05.24sec.

Also in the pool, Brazilian Cesar Filho Cielo claimed his second medal of the Games with a surprise victory in the 50m freestyle to add to the bronze he won in the 100m.

Britain continued their dominance in the cycling with Chris Hoy taking his second gold of the Games and Bradley Wiggins his first. Scotsman Hoy eased to victory in the keirin ahead of teammate Ross Edgar, while Wiggins defeated New Zealand's Hayden Roulston to win the men's individual pursuit with another Briton, youngster Steven Burke, taking bronze.

Spain stemmed the British tide of success with Joan Llaneras winning the

British pair Chris Hoy (top) and Ross Edgar celebrate their gold and silver medals in the keirin

Valeriy Borchin heads for victory in the 20km walk, Russia's first track and field gold of the Games

points race, but the Union Jack still got an airing with Chris Newton finishing third. And Dave Brailsford's record-breaking team ensured at least one more gold when Rebecca Romero and Wendy Houvenaghel posted the two fastest qualifying times in the women's pursuit, setting up an all-British final.

A stunned Hoy admitted the success of the team made it hard to concentrate. 'To finish with one-two on the podium, that's just unbelievable,' he said. 'There are so many things going on around you. Bradley and Steven coming first and third was just incredible, the girls getting one and two in the final tomorrow, and Chris winning the bronze in the points, it's been such an amazing day for the team, but you have to focus on your ride and not think about the stuff that's happening around you.'

The fourth British gold of the day came in the rowing, where the flagship men's four produced a superb final 250m to overhaul Australia – the third successive British win in the event but the first without Sir Steve Redgrave or Sir Matthew Pinsent.

Other golds on the lake were spread around with Bulgaria's Rumyana Neykova and Olaf Tufte of Norway taking the honours in the single sculls while Romania's Georgeta Andrunache and Viorica Susanu took the women's

pair gold medal before Australians Duncan Free and Drew Ginn emphatically clinched the men's title.

Australia won their second gold medal of the regatta with victory in the men's double sculls for Scott Brennan and David Crawshay.

Back at the Bird's Nest, Valeriy Borchin earned a surprise victory in the 20km walk to win Russia their first gold medal of the track and field programme. Borchin's surge over the last 4km put him clear of the challenge of Ecuador's reigning world champion, Jefferson Perez, by 14 seconds.

The heptathlon title went to Nataliya Dobrynska of Ukraine, who passed overnight leader Hyleas Fountain of the United States to win with a total of 6,733 points. New Zealand's Valerie

Great Britain's triumphant
men's four of Tom James,
Steve Williams, Pete Reed and
Andrew Triggs-Hodge

Vili won the women's shot put final with a throw of 20.56m.

Roger Federer's quest for an Olympic gold medal came to fruition, although not in the way anyone expected. The struggling Swiss had already been knocked out of the singles by James Blake, but he and compatriot Stanislas Wawrinka took the doubles title with a 6–3 6–4 6–7 (4/7) 6–3 victory over Swedes Simon Aspelin and Thomas Johansson. American favourites Bob and Mike Bryan had to settle for bronze.

Oleksandr Petriv of the Ukraine took gold in the men's 25m rapid fire pistol with a new Olympic-record score of 780.2, while in the last shotgun event of the Games, 19-year-old American shooter Vincent Hancock won gold in the men's skeet in a shoot-off.

Zhang Ning defended her women's badminton singles title, defeating Chinese compatriot Xie Xingfang, while Indonesian duo Hendra Setiawan and Markis Kido defeated Cai Yun and Fu Haifeng of China to clinch the men's doubles gold medal, eight years after their first Olympic title.

Jang Mi-ran of South Korea broke three world records in taking gold in the women's weightlifting +75kg class, while Carol Huynh took Canada's first Beijing gold in the women's freestyle 48kg wrestling. ■

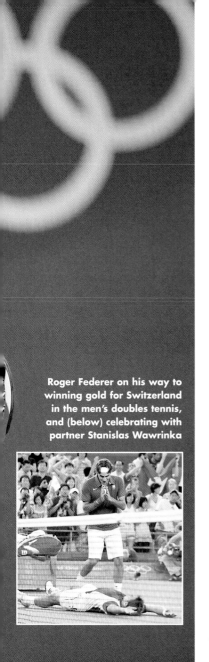

Roger Federer on his way to winning gold for Switzerland in the men's doubles tennis, and (below) celebrating with partner Stanislas Wawrinka

Michael Phelps is the centre of attention but manages to find mother Debbie and sister Whitney as he celebrates completing a record eight gold medals in a single Games (inset above)

The morning after Usain Bolt had blazed across the 100m finish line in audacious isolation, Michael Phelps drew on the help of three teammates and the will of the sporting world to reclaim the headlines and enhance his place in history.

Where Bolt had beaten his chest and launched himself on a solitary lap of honour, Phelps embraced the 4x100m medley relay partners who had ensured he would realise his dream of claiming eight gold medals in one Games, surpassing the great Mark Spitz.

'What else could I do?' grinned Phelps after claiming that eighth and last Beijing gold medal while he stood on the pool deck, watching Jason Lezak touch first to set a new world record, Phelps' seventh of the Games.

The American's fantastic achievement reverberated around his sport and way beyond.

'I'm privileged to see Michael Phelps win eight gold medals,' said Australian Leisel Jones, herself a double gold medallist at the Games. 'It's an honour to be here in the same era. I couldn't care less about my own swims. Him winning eight gold medals is pretty amazing.'

Phelps' quest for swimming immortality became a reality when the American quartet – completed by Aaron

Michael Phelps shares the glory with teammates Brendan Hansen (left), Aaron Peirsol (third left) and Jason Lezak (right) after completing his set of eight gold medals with victory in the 4x100m medley relay. The start of the race is pictured right

Peirsol, Brendan Hansen and Lezak – touched the wall in 3min 29.34sec, 1.34sec under the world record.

'It's all a dream come true,' added Phelps. 'This is something we have been looking forward to for four years. It's been fun for the last four years and it's been one fun week, that's for sure.'

The men's relay result was a reversal of the top two positions in the women's race, with Australia taking gold ahead of the United States.

In an action-packed day of swimming, Grant Hackett's bid for a historic treble in the 1500m freestyle was ended by Tunisian Oussama Mellouli, who relegated the Australian

to second place for the first time at any Olympics.

Britta Steffen, meanwhile, completed the freestyle sprint double by winning the 50m in a time of 24.06sec, defeating 41-year-old veteran Dara Torres of the United States.

On the track, Shelly-Ann Fraser followed compatriot Bolt and led an unprecedented Jamaican clean sweep to claim gold in the women's 100m. Teammates Sherone Simpson and Kerron Stewart could not be separated after a lengthy study of a photo finish, and were both awarded silver medals.

Kenenisa Bekele confirmed his position as the greatest long-distance track runner of his generation by successfully defending his 10,000m crown. The event also marked possibly the last Olympic appearance of Bekele's compatriot and former two-time champion over the distance, Haile Gebrselassie, who came home a creditable sixth.

Veteran Romanian Constantina Tomescu-Dita took a surprise gold in the women's marathon. The 38-year-old came home in a time of 2hr, 26min and 44sec with Kenyan Catherine Ndereba claiming silver, edging China's Zhou Chunxiu into bronze position after a battle down the home straight. World record-holder Paula Radcliffe limped home in 23rd after rushing her recovery from a fractured femur – another Olympic disappointment following her failure to finish in Athens.

Russia's Gulnara Galkina-Samitova broke her own world record to win the inaugural Olympic 3,000m women's steeplechase. The 30-year-old Russian pulled clear of the field with three laps left to run, and went on to better her own four-year-old mark with a new time of 8min, 58.81sec.

Rafael Nadal celebrated his imminent rise to the top of the tennis world rankings by becoming Olympic champion with victory over Chilean Fernando Gonzalez in the men's singles. The Olympics are traditionally

seen as less important than the grand slams to tennis players, but Nadal insisted: 'Here I feel like I won it for my whole country, not just for myself. So that makes it a little bit more special.'

Elena Dementieva overcame a familiar attack of nerves to end Darina Safina's 15-match winning streak and triumph 3–6 7–5 6–3 in the women's singles, while Vera Zvonareva's bronze medal ensured a Russian clean sweep. Dementieva said: 'To win a gold medal is unbelievable. I have been dreaming of this moment since I was eight years old.'

Venus and Serena Williams teamed up to win the women's doubles with a surprisingly easy win over Spain's

Kenenisa Bekele celebrates winning the 10,000m (above) for the second successive Olympic Games

Venus and Serena Williams celebrate gold for the United States in the women's doubles tennis

Anabel Medina-Garrigues and Virginia Ruano Pascual.

Great Britain won a gold and two silvers as they took their overall medal total in the rowing to six, finishing the regatta as the top nation. Zac Purchase and Mark Hunter took gold in the lightweight men's double sculls, while Britain also took silver in the men's eight and women's quadruple sculls.

Canada won their first gold of the regatta when their men claimed victory in the closing eights, with the United States taking the title in the women's eights. Poland clinched gold in the

men's quadruple sculls, with Denmark taking the lightweight men's fours and the Netherlands claiming the women's double sculls.

Britain's success on the water continued in the sailing as they carried off the gold medals in the Yngling – through Sarah Ayton, Sarah Webb and Pippa Wilson – and Finn classes, with a third successive gold for Ben Ainslie.

And there was yet more success in the cycling for Team GB as Rebecca Romero became the first British woman to win medals in two different sports when she beat compatriot Wendy

Sarah Ayton, Sarah Webb and Pippa Wilson head for gold for Great Britain in the Yngling class

France beat the United States in the men's team sabre final

Houvenaghel in the final of the pursuit. Romero had taken a rowing silver medal in Athens, but may still have ambitions in cycling after being inspired by the multiple successes of her teammates. 'I think now I can relax and be content, just see the limits I can push myself to as a bike rider, see if I can be like Bradley Wiggins or Chris Hoy because that would be the ultimate,' she said.

China claimed double gold in the gymnastics as Xiao Qin took the men's pommel horse title and Zou Kai added the floor exercise, while the hosts also won their fifth diving medal out of five as defending champion Guo Jingjing retained her title in the women's 3m springboard.

Japan's Icho Kaori comfortably out-wrestled Russia's Alena Kartashova in the 63kg freestyle category, while China's Wang Jiao won the 72kg.

France took the final gold medal in fencing by beating the United States in the men's team sabre final, and Ilya Ilin of Kazakhstan won the men's 94kg weightlifting with a total lift of 406kg.

There was no doubt, however, who the day belonged to.

'His level of achievement is phenomenal,' said Australian icon Grant Hackett as the world stood back in awe and admired Phelps. ■

Zou Kai takes gold for China in the floor exercise

The hopes of more than a billion people rested on the shoulders of Liu Xiang, but there was to be no 'Cathy Freeman moment' for China at Beijing 2008.

Liu, defending Olympic champion, national icon and poster boy of the Games, was supposed to deliver track gold in front of an adoring Bird's Nest crowd. But those dreams turned to an ocean of tears when Liu pulled out of his 110m hurdles heat with an injury.

Fans across China, the national media and Liu's coach, Sun Haiping, all broke down as they tried to come to terms with the crushing disappointment of his withdrawal. The Chinese superstar had aggravated a long-standing injury to his right Achilles tendon – his take-off foot – during training and he was described as being in 'intolerable' pain by the time he took to the track.

The race began with a false start but just the movement out of the starting blocks was too much for Liu to bear. He ripped off his numbers, limped down the tunnel and out of the National Stadium.

The 90,000-strong crowd crammed inside the stadium let out an anguished cry when the announcement was made that their hero had withdrawn from the competition. Liu had been expected to

Coach Sun Haiping is in tears (above) after national hero Liu Xiang is forced to withdraw from the 110m hurdles (below and opposite)

go head-to-head with Cuban world record-holder Dayron Robles and win on home soil – just as Australian track star Freeman had done in the 400m at Sydney 2000 – in what would have been the highlight of the Games for the host nation.

One star of the track and field programme who did live up to expectations was Russian pole vault world record-holder Yelena Isinbayeva, who won gold to defend her Olympic title and went on to set a world record of 5.05m.

Ever the entertainer, she hid beneath a large white duvet-like sheet before taking three attempts at shaving a centimetre off her own world mark. When she succeeded on her final vault she was celebrating well before she hit the landing cushion. Incredibly, it was the 24th world record Isinbayeva had set in her discipline. The Russian required just two vaults to take the gold, the crucial one measuring 4.85m, or a foot and a half higher than your average London bus.

As the rest of the field battled through the early rounds, Isinbayeva joined the competition one hour and 30 minutes in, entering at 4.70m with American rival Jennifer Stuczynski leading from Svetlana Feofanova. One by one, however, Isinbayeva's rivals went out –

teammate Feofanova in tears, although in the bronze medal position. At that point Isinbayeva re-entered the fray in the most majestic fashion, muttering at the pole in trademark fashion on the runway before soaring over the bar at 4.85m. When Stuczynski could not manage 4.90m with her three attempts, the gold was Isinbayeva's.

There followed 45 minutes of pure theatre as the Russian sought inspiration under her duvet before eventually

creating the biggest roar of the night. 'I felt that I could not go out without the world record because of the support the crowd gave me,' she explained afterwards.

Angelo Taylor led a United States clean sweep of the men's 400m hurdles with a personal-best time. Taylor crossed the line in 47.25sec to add Beijing gold to the one he won in the same event at Sydney 2000. Kerron Clement took the silver medal in a time

Yelena Isinbayeva screams with joy after setting an amazing 24th world record to win the gold for Russia in the women's pole vault (above)

Great Britain head for victory in the cycling team pursuit final against Denmark

of 47.98sec, with Bershawn Jackson claiming bronze.

There was double success for Kenya as Pamela Jelimo claimed their first-ever women's athletics gold medal when she won the 800m. The 18-year-old crossed the line well clear of compatriot Janeth Jepkosgei Busienei. And the African nation was celebrating again when Brimin Kiprop Kipruto won their seventh successive 3,000m steeplechase gold.

Reigning world champion Irving Jahir Saladino Aranda became Panama's first athletics gold medallist in the men's long jump, while the United States' Stephanie Brown Trafton outclassed the field to win the women's discus with a throw of

64.74m in the opening round of the competition.

Great Britain's Bradley Wiggins won his second gold of the Games in the cycling team pursuit as he, Geraint Thomas, Ed Clancy and Paul Manning shattered their own world record in beating Denmark.

Also in the velodrome, Marianne Vos of Holland won gold in the women's points race.

Australia's Emma Snowsill destroyed the rest of the field with a devastating running leg to win the women's triathlon, while at Qingdao, Denmark were eventually confirmed as winners of the sailing 49er class. The mast of the

Beijing 2008

Brimin Kiprop Kipruto (2285) bides his time in the middle of the field on his way to winning the 3,000m steeplechase

Danish boat snapped before the start of their race, forcing them to borrow a boat from Croatia, in which they came seventh. That was good enough to give them the gold medal, but the race committee questioned the replacement of their boat. However, the jury subsequently threw the protest out and upheld the race result.

Despite a ninth-place finish in the medal race, Australia's Elise Rechichi and Tessa Parkinson won the women's 470 class, matching the success of the Australian men's 470 pair of Nathan Wilmot and Malcolm Page.

He Kexin won China's seventh gymnastics gold of the Games as she held off Nastia Liukin in the uneven bars after both scored 16.725. The home favourite took the honours because she had made fewer mistakes.

Polish gymnast Leszek Blanik claimed the men's vault over France's Thomas Bouhail on a tiebreak, Chen Yibing took the gold in the men's rings and He Wenna won the trampoline gold.

China won the men's table tennis as the trio of Wang Hao, Ma Lin and Wang Liqin beat Germany 3–0, while at the equestrian base in Hong Kong, the United States claimed a nailbiting victory via a jump-off against Canada after both finished with 20 penalty points.

Chen Yibing shows the strain as he wins gold for China in the men's rings

Christine
Ohuruogu
beams with
delight after
victory for
Great Britain
in the 400m
(opposite)

Christine Ohuruogu and Chris Hoy led the celebrations on a golden day for Great Britain, which ended with a flurry of medals.

Ohuruogu became the first British woman to win the Olympic 400m title when she produced a storming finish to overhaul favourite Sanya Richards. But it was cyclist Hoy who really captured the imagination of the public back home, as he struck gold for a third time by beating teammate Jason Kenny in the men's sprint at the Laoshan Velodrome.

Scot Hoy was pushed to the limit in the first race by his 20-year-old opponent but edged the opening duel in the best-of-three series by half a wheel's length. However, in the second race he was completely dominant and had enough of a lead to give a victory salute as he crossed the line.

Hoy's achievement made him only the second Briton ever to claim three golds in one Games – swimmer Henry Taylor was the other in London in 1908.

'It's the most unbelievable feeling,' Hoy said. 'I feel great to be one of the medal winners this time. You cross the line and all the pressure and expectation evaporates and it's like nothing else you've ever felt. It's about the process and the performance, breaking it down to the technical elements. That's why the emotions come

out at the end; it just erupts out of you. To have a gold medal to chalk up there for Team GB is a great feeling.'

Hoy's success made him the poster-boy of Britain's Games, but just a few moments earlier it was teammate Victoria Pendleton who had shown him the way with a superb ride to win the women's sprint.

The 27-year-old beat Anna Meares of Australia in the final with a display that was a long way from the moment when she froze on the Olympic stage four years previously in Athens. She had finished sixth in the now absent time trial in Greece and was knocked out in the first round of the sprint.

There was no such disappointment this time, however, and Pendleton was quick to praise the part sports psychologist Steve Peters had played in helping to develop her winning mentality. She said: 'I honestly don't think I'd be here if it wasn't for Steve Peters.

'I've wanted this so badly. I'd beaten everyone in the field, so there was a lot of pressure on me to win a medal – I'm "the golden girl of the track". But I didn't think about the outcome, I just tried to focus on the process. I didn't even allow myself to think about winning or failing, I just focused on the training I'd done.'

There was some disappointment for Britain's cyclists in the madison, when

Chris Hoy completes his hat-trick of cycling gold medals in the sprint

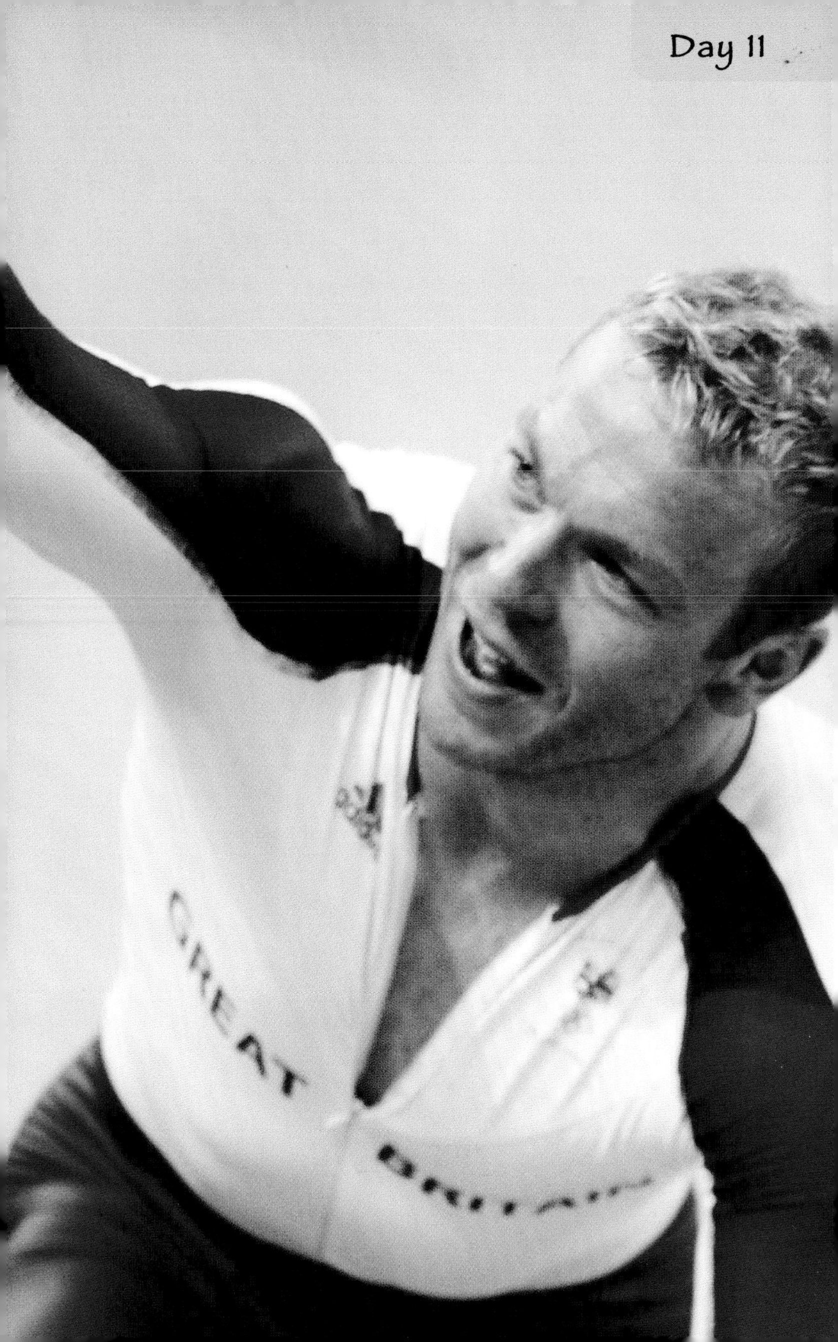
GREAT

Bradley Wiggins failed to match Hoy in claiming a third gold medal of the Games, but events at the Bird's Nest soon erased that.

Germaine Mason had already taken silver in the high jump with a leap of 2.34m – equalling his personal best behind eventual winner Andrey Silnov – when Ohuruogu stormed to victory on the track. Favourite Richards insisted a hamstring injury was the reason she tied up badly down the home straight as she could only finish third.

Ohuruogu added Olympic gold to the world title she won in Osaka in 2007, saying: 'I have come here and got what I wanted and I'm happy. I had a race plan but, as usual, it went out of the window. All I had to work off was the Russian girl outside me, who I knew would go off very hard, and at 200m I was annoyed with myself that I had left myself too much work.'

Elsewhere, there was drama in the women's 100m hurdles as Lolo Jones blew her chance of victory. The American looked to have the race won before she hit the penultimate hurdle and stumbled to seventh. Teammate Dawn Harper took advantage to win with Australian Sally McLellan taking the silver medal ahead of Canada's Priscilla Lopes-Schliep after a photo-finish.

There was also a thrilling finish in the triathlon as Germany's Jan Frodeno burst past Sydney champion Simon Whitfield to win his first Olympic title. New Zealander Bevan Docherty took the bronze medal. Meanwhile, Bahrain's Rashid Ramzi showed nerves of steel to win the 1500m title and, in

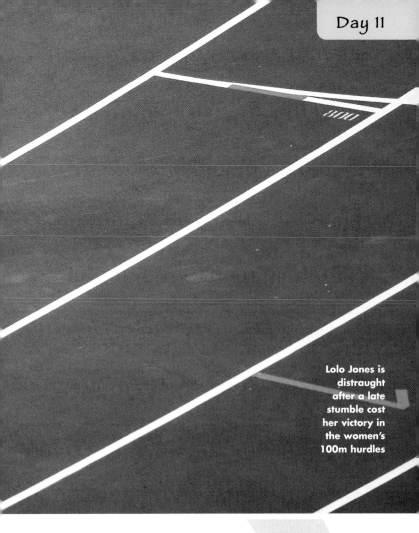

Lolo Jones is distraught after a late stumble cost her victory in the women's 100m hurdles

the field, Gerd Kanter added the Olympic discus gold to his collection with a winning throw of 68.82m.

Day 11 also saw further success for hosts China. The home nation had plenty to celebrate as Li Xiaopeng won his fourth Olympic gold in the men's parallel bars and Lu Chunlong won their first Olympic trampoline gold in the men's competition. Zou Kai also took gold in the horizontal bar while Chinese domination of the diving continued when He Chong won the men's 3m springboard.

Germany's Matthias Steiner won the men's +105kg weightlifting and dedicated his victory to the memory of wife Susann, who died in a car crash in 2007. Favourite Mavlet Batirov of Russia won the men's freestyle 60kg wrestling with victory over Vasyl Fedoryshyn of the Ukraine, while Henry Cejudo of the United States took gold in the 55kg class after beating Japan's Matsunaga Tomohiro.

There were also medals decided in the sailing at Qingdao, where Britain's Paul Goodison made up for missing out on Olympic glory four years previously with victory in the Laser class.

Goodison only needed to avoid finishing last in the 10-boat race to take the honours and, in the light winds of the Yellow Sea, he opted to err on the side of caution. He covered Sweden's Rasmus Myrgren – the only man who could have denied him the gold medal – from the start, and in the end a ninth-place finish proved to be enough.

Also at Qingdao, Anna Tunnicliffe gave the United States their first sailing gold with a second-place finish behind Lithuania's Gintare Volungeviciute in the medal race for the Laser Radial.

The 25-year-old was ninth midway through the race but stormed back to finish just behind Volungeviciute, who took the silver.

Paul Goodison celebrates victory for Great Britain in the Laser class

Germany's Matthias Steiner on his way to victory in the men's +105kg weightlifting

Usain Bolt completed his ascent to athletics and Olympic greatness with the outstanding performance of day 12.

Before the Games began, the Jamaican was recognised in athletics circles as a phenomenon with talent to burn, and with his 100m gold medal and world record he became a worldwide household name.

But his performance in the 200m was nothing short of sensational – for he smashed the world record that many expected to last a lifetime.

Michael Johnson ran 19.32sec in Atlanta 12 years previously, taking an astonishing four-tenths of a second off Pietro Mennea's 17-year-old world record in the space of one Games.

No one went close to Johnson's time in the subsequent dozen years, but Bolt had the Beijing Bird's Nest crowd watching in awe as he went for glory from the gun.

A brilliant run off the bend put him far clear of the rest of the field, and Bolt showed no sign of easing off – as he did in the 100m final – as he powered through the line to stop the clock showing 19.31sec.

Another hundredth of a second was shaved off the time when the official results came through as Bolt established a new world record of 19.30sec.

The Jamaican became the first athlete since Carl Lewis in Los Angeles in 1984 to win the men's Olympic sprint double, and in the process he added a new chapter to the sprinting history books.

It was a perfect way to start the celebrations for his birthday, with his second gold coming a day before he turned 22. 'This is more than I can handle really, I'm a bit overwhelmed,'

Usain Bolt celebrates his second
spectacular sprint gold medal

Day 12

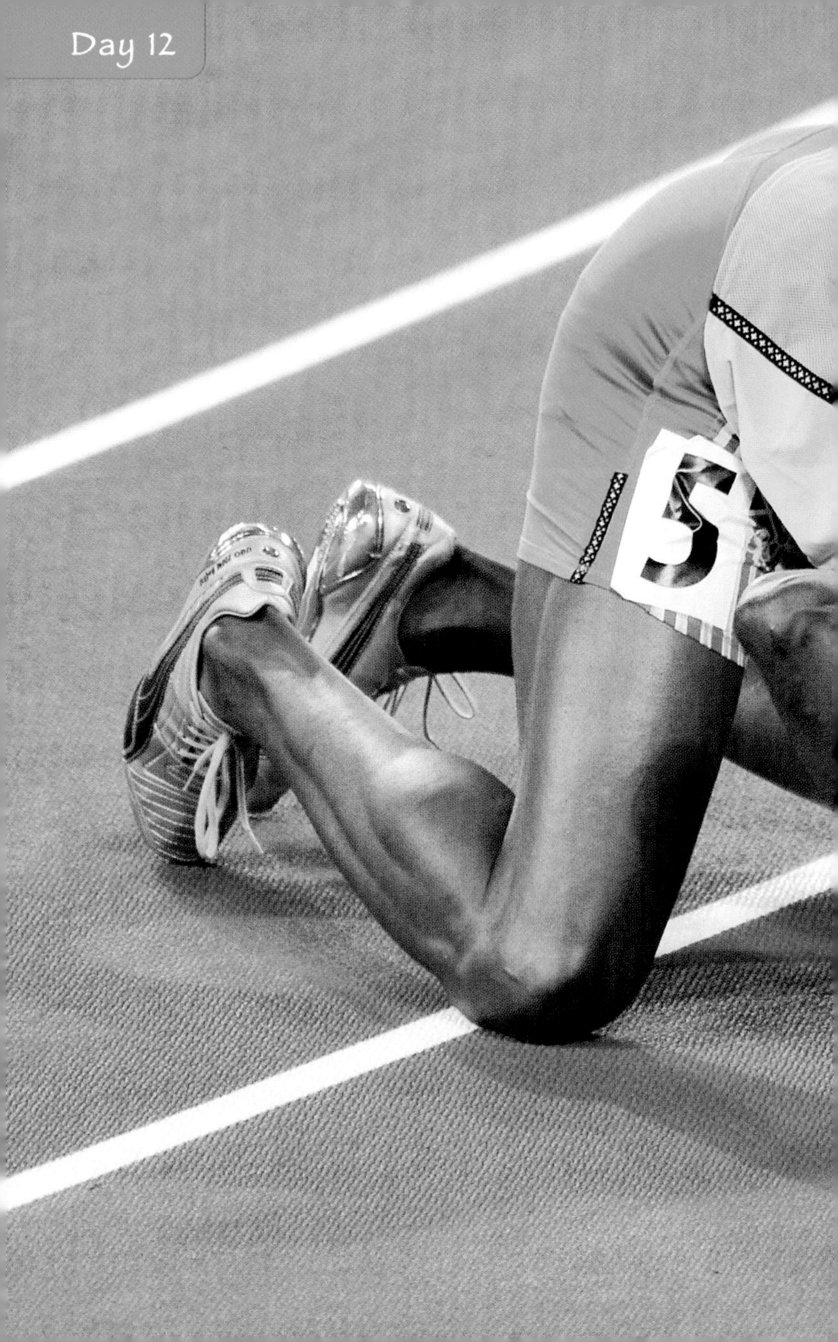

Bolt said. 'I didn't think a 200m record was on, because I felt tired after the heats. But I told everyone I was going to come out here and leave everything on the track and I did just that. I've proved I'm a true champion and that you can do anything you want with hard work. It's great. I have a great feeling. This is a dream come true.'

Churandy Martina of the Dutch Antilles and American Wallace Spearmon were initially credited with silver and bronze, only for both to be disqualified for running outside their lanes. That handed American Shawn Crawford the silver medal with teammate Walter Dix claiming the bronze.

Before Bolt's dramatic triumph, the first athletics gold medal of the evening had gone to Aksana Miankova of Belarus, whose hammer throw of 76.34m gave her a new Olympic record.

Cuba's Yipsi Moreno, runner-up in Athens in 2004, again had to settle for the silver medal after a best effort of 75.20m, while China's Zhang Wenxiu delighted another 90,000-strong crowd by claiming bronze with 74.32m.

Miankova said: 'This is my first gold medal. I felt I was so successful tonight.'

In the final athletics event of the evening, Jamaica's Melaine Walker won gold in the 400m hurdles in a new Olympic record of 52.64sec.

Walker powered off the final hurdle to finish comfortably ahead of American Sheena Tosta, with Britain's Natasha Danvers snatching bronze. 'I was kind of expecting it,' Walker said. 'I've dreamed about it a million times.'

Russia's multiple world champion Larisa Ilchenko took victory in the final women's swimming event of the Games

Larisa Ilchenko
heads for
victory in the
10km open
water swim,
ahead of
British pair
Keri-Anne
Payne and
Cassie Patten

when she came out on top in a sprint finish in the 10km open water race. Ilchenko crossed the finishing line in a time of 1hr 59min 27.7sec, to deny British pair Keri-Anne Payne and Cassie Patten, who had led for the majority of the race. Ilchenko, who defeated Patten at the death during the World Championships in Melbourne last year, adopted her usual tactic of sitting just behind the leading pair, allowing the

British duo to pull her through the water with the minimum of effort.

With 250m to go, the Russian pulled alongside the front two but Payne fought back, matching her stroke for stroke until, almost inevitably, Ilchenko inched ahead to touch ahead of Payne with Patten taking bronze.

Ilchenko said: 'I was trying to convince myself that this was a training swim, that it was a 10km trial that I had

Yin Jian wins the women's RS:X windsurfing to earn China's first Olympic gold in sailing

to win. I had to equate it to a training session, and I finally won against these great athletes.'

Yin Jian won China's first-ever Olympic sailing gold when she triumphed in the women's RS:X windsurfing, ahead of Italy's Alessandra Sensini and Great Britain's Bryony Shaw.

World champion Tom Ashley of New Zealand landed gold in the men's RS:X by just a point from Julien Bontemps of France. Shahar Zubari won Israel's first medal of the Games in securing bronze.

Turkey also claimed their first medal of the Games when Ramazan Sahin struck gold with victory over Ukraine's Andriy Stadnik in the men's 66kg wrestling event.

Buvaysa Saytiev claimed Russia's fifth wrestling gold by defeating Soslan Tigiev of Uzbekistan 0–1 1–0 3–1 in the men's freestyle 74kg category.

Anastasia Davydova and Anastasia Ermakova, also of Russia, made it a hat-trick of Olympic titles in the synchronised swimming duet, ahead of their Spanish and Japanese rivals.

There was another Chinese gold for the hosts to celebrate in taekwondo, as Wu Jingyu defeated Buttree Puedpong of Thailand in the women's -49kg category. Mexican Guillermo Perez later claimed the gold medal in the

Ramazan Sahin (top) wins Turkey's first medal of the Games as he wins the 66kg wrestling final

men's -58kg class by defeating Yulis Gabriel Mercedes of the Dominican Republic, while Rohullah Nikpai of Afghanistan took bronze to become the first person from his country to win an Olympic medal.

There was sour news amid all the glory, though, with the announcement that heptathlon silver medallist Lyudmila Blonska had failed a drugs test for the second time in her career.

The International Olympic Committee later confirmed the Ukrainian had been 'removed from the Olympic Games' and stripped of her medal. ■

Another day, another opportunity for Jamaica's sprinters to demonstrate their supremacy over the United States in the Bird's Nest Stadium. And on day 13 of the Olympic Games, American folly was almost as responsible as Jamaican brilliance for maintaining the trend of Caribbean superiority.

The Olympic 4x100m relay semi-finals are where professionalism should kick in to ensure safe passage to the final but, incredibly, both the US men's and women's teams dropped their batons and crashed out.

They had both seemed certain to win medals, with the only obstacle being their ability to carry the baton the full one-lap distance. However, Tyson Gay and Darvis Patton failed to negotiate the men's final exchange, and Torri Edwards and Lauryn Williams made a mess of the last changeover for the women's sprint quartet.

As Jamaica eased through to both finals, the Americans were left to reflect on their failures. World 100m champion Gay, who surprisingly failed to make the final of the individual 100m in Beijing, could not hide his disappointment.

He said: 'It is probably my fault. I am going to take the blame for it. I have never dropped a stick in my life. It is just

The baton falls to the ground between Tyson Gay and Darvis Patton and the Americans are out of the 4x100m relay at the semi-final stage

Veronica Campbell-Brown celebrates after winning the women's 200m final (opposite)

the way it has been happening for me this year.'

Williams was visibly shaken by the women's team crashing out. She said: 'I really don't know what happened, I guess I dropped the stick. I thought my hand was there, maybe someone has a voodoo doll of me. If people want to blame me they can blame, I don't care. It's definitely very humbling for Team USA, and we're going to hold our head high and get through it.'

Veronica Campbell-Brown anchored the Jamaican team to their semi-final victory just 90 minutes after landing the individual 200m.

After Usain Bolt smashed Michael Johnson's world record in the men's 200m on the Wednesday, Thursday saw Campbell-Brown follow her fellow Jamaican into Beijing's gold medal ranks. For Campbell-Brown, it was a second Olympic 200m gold after her triumph in Athens four years earlier. On this occasion, she powered to the line in a new personal best of 21.74sec. American Allyson Felix followed her Athens silver with another runner-up finish.

With euphoria sweeping through the Jamaican squad, Campbell-Brown was determined not to let anybody down. Shortly after the race, she admitted: 'There was some pressure, there was a

LaShawn Merritt enjoys the attention after winning 400m gold

lot of motivation from my team, but fear is not something I bring to the track.'

There was at least an American 1-2-3 in the men's 400m, although not in the expected order, as defending champion Jeremy Wariner was surprisingly beaten into second place by teammate LaShawn Merritt. Wariner had been tipped in some quarters to challenge

Michael Johnson's 400m world record.

World record-holder Dayron Robles duly won the 110m hurdles, but the absence of injured Chinese superstar Liu Xiang meant it was a race lacking its anticipated lustre.

Triple-jump glory went to Portugal's Nelson Evora, who defeated gold medal favourite Phillips Idowu, with the

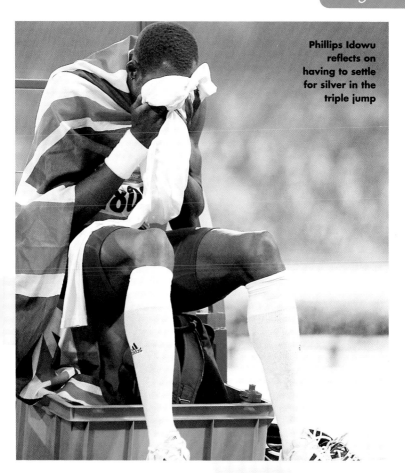

Phillips Idowu reflects on having to settle for silver in the triple jump

Briton having to settle for silver.

Away from a busy day in track and field, there was a notable victory for leukaemia survivor Maarten van der Weijden of Holland in the inaugural men's 10km open water swim.

Van der Weijden got the better of David Davies of Great Britain and Thomas Lurz of Germany to win in a time of 1hr 51min 51.6sec at the rain-swept Shunyi Olympic Rowing-Canoeing Park.

'The leukaemia has taught me to think step-by-step,' said Van der Weijden. 'When you are in hospital and feeling so much pain and feeling so tired, you don't want to think about the next day or week – you just think about the next

Iain Percy and
Andrew Simpson win
gold for Great Britain
in the Star class

Americans Misty May-Treanor and Kerri Walsh celebrate their beach volleyball gold

hour. It teaches you to be patient when you are lying in a hospital bed, and that was almost the same strategy I chose here to wait for my chance in the pack.'

Russia's Olga Kaniskina claimed the gold medal in the women's 20km walk, and British sailors Iain Percy and Andrew Simpson celebrated becoming Olympic champions in the Star class, while Fernando Echavarri and Anton Paz of Spain took gold in the Tornado class.

Six minutes into extra-time Carli Lloyd scored the only goal of the final as the United States women's football team beat Brazil. Reflecting on her achievement later, Lloyd said: 'Truly, it was an amazing moment when I scored that goal, but the best moment was standing up on that podium receiving that gold medal and knowing we did it together and we believed in each other.'

America landed another gold in the women's beach volleyball. Defending champions Misty May-Treanor and Kerri Walsh retained their title after overcoming China's Tian Jia and Wang Jie in straight sets.

Russian Andrey Moiseev could go for a hat-trick of modern pentathlon golds in 2012 after mounting a successful defence of his Athens title in Beijing. He claimed the gold with 5,632 points, ahead of Lithuanians Edvinas Krungolcas and Andrejus Zadneprovskis, who took silver and bronze.

South Koreans Son Tae-jin and Lim Su-jeong took golds in taekwondo, while Uzbekistan's Artur Taymazov defended his freestyle 120kg wrestling title and Russian Shirvani Muradov prevailed in the 96kg category.

A special Olympic moment for Tajikistan arrived when wrestler Yusup Abdusalomov won his country's first-ever silver medal, losing out to Georgia's Revazi Mindorashvili for gold in the 84kg category.

China's dominant diving performance continued as Chen Ruolin won the women's 10m platform.

Holland won the women's water polo gold, and Japan triumphed in softball. Silver, on both occasions went to the United States.

They may not have won gold, but at least the American softball team did not drop the bat when it mattered. ∎

Tirunesh Dibaba of Ethiopia (inset right) follows her 10,000m gold with victory in the 5,000m

The new king and queen of athletics were crowned on an electric night in the Bird's Nest as Ethiopia's Tirunesh Dibaba and Jamaican Usain Bolt added to their medal collection in spectacular fashion.

Dibaba became the first woman to complete the long-distance double with victory in the 5,000m, while Bolt stormed to his third gold medal of the Games in the 4x100m relay.

The 23-year-old Dibaba edged Turkey's Elvan Abeylegesse by a second to add to her 10,000m success earlier in the Games. She said: 'It's a big achievement for me. When I came from my country I didn't think I'd win both. I just thought I'd be a good competitor in both events. Now that I have it, I'm quite satisfied.'

Meanwhile, Jamaica obliterated the field in the men's 4x100m relay as Bolt claimed his third gold and world record of the Beijing Games.

The quartet of Bolt, Nesta Carter, Michael Frater and Asafa Powell roared around the track to shave three tenths of a second off the 15-year-old mark with a blistering time of 37.10sec.

Bolt, the individual 100m and 200m champion, was instrumental in the victory after running a stunning third leg as the team finished well clear of Trinidad and Tobago and Japan. 'You

can't really explain the feeling after the greatest Olympics ever, so I'm happy,' insisted Bolt.

He continued: 'All I can say is Jamaican sprinters are taking over the world. We've always been the sprinters, but we're going to tell the world we're taking over forever.'

The win was far from a solo effort, though, as former 100m world record-holder Powell recovered from finishing fifth in the 100m final to bring home gold on the final leg. Powell relished the chance for redemption and hailed the impact of his teammates.

'It's something that I'm used to, you know? But, being with a team, it's different,' Powell said when referring to breaking the relay record.

Frater, who established the Jamaicans' advantage on the second leg, was bullish about his nation's chances of dominating the sport.

'37.10 [seconds], smashing the record, I think it's going to take something special to break this record. But I think next year, we'll break it,' he beamed. 'Next time, 36 [seconds].'

Elsewhere in the stadium, Maurren Maggi made history by becoming the first Brazilian athlete to win a field event. Her opening 7.04m effort was enough to seal gold in the women's long jump. 'I just wanted a medal, I didn't care what colour it was,' she revealed. 'I was so moved to hear the music of the Brazilian national anthem on the podium. I'd like to share this medal with people who helped me a lot, especially my family, my friends and my daughter.'

Back on the track, Jamaica's women could not follow the success of their men as they threw away the women's 4x100m relay gold when they dropped the baton on the penultimate changeover. It was a rare moment of misfortune for Jamaica's sprinters, who were dominant over short distances throughout the Games. With the

Asafa Powell leads home the Jamaican 4x100m relay team and (below) celebrates with teammates Usain Bolt, Michael Frater and Nesta Carter

Russia win the women's 4x100m relay ahead of Belgium and Nigeria

favourites out, Russia claimed the title for the first time, clocking 42.31sec, while Belgium posted a national record of 42.54sec to earn silver, with Nigeria coming in third.

Aleksandra Fedoriva of the Russian quartet revealed the victory was beyond their wildest dreams. She said: 'We would have been happy with a silver medal, but we got the gold!'

Bryan Clay took the honours in the men's decathlon, while Steve Hooper of Australia won pole vault gold with a new Olympic record.

In Laoshan, Latvia's Maris Strombergs kept a cool head to celebrate a narrow victory in the men's BMX. He grabbed the lead in the first corner and rode with confidence to win the title on the sport's maiden Olympic outing.

Anne-Caroline Chausson of France took gold in the women's event as favourite Shanaze Reade of Great Britain crashed out.

Home interest was centred at the Peking University Gymnasium, where China's women's singles table tennis players claimed a clean sweep of gold, silver and bronze medals in line with their world ranking heading into the Games.

World number one Zhang Yining beat teammate Wang Nan 4–2 to win the gold medal, while Guo Yue

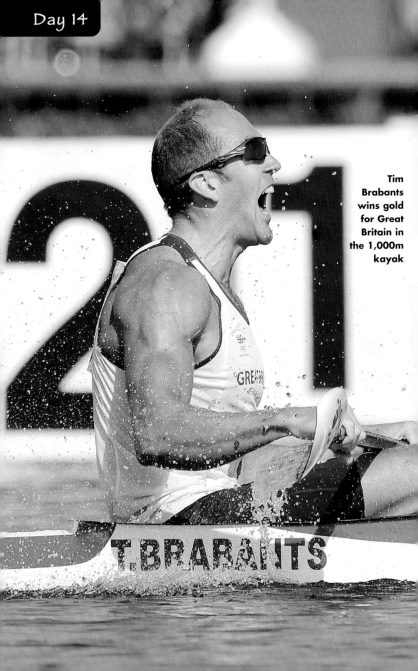

Tim Brabants wins gold for Great Britain in the 1,000m kayak

Dutch hockey captain Minke Booij celebrates adding gold to her silver and bronze medals from past Games

overcame Singapore's Li Jiawei to claim the bronze.

However, the hosts were not so successful in the women's hockey final. China made their first appearance in the showpiece against the Netherlands, but they were unable to celebrate the landmark with a victory. Naomi van As scored the opening goal before Maartje Goderie scored the decisive second to give the Dutch their first Olympic women's hockey gold since 1984.

'It's my third Olympics. I won bronze in Sydney, silver in Athens and now gold. It's a perfect way to go,' enthused captain Minke Booij.

In another historic feat, Tim Brabants became British canoeing's first Olympic champion with a comfortable win in the 1,000m kayak single final. The 31-year-old doctor, already world and European title-holder, led from start to finish ahead of Norway's defending champion Eirik Larsen.

'It is fantastic,' said Brabants. 'I was very happy last year to win the World Championships – it was the first time a British athlete has done it in 20 years. Now this is the first time a British athlete has won a gold medal in the sport of kayak racing.'

In other events on the water, Germany's Martin Hollstein and Andreas Ihle won the kayak double 100m race while there was more golden glory for Germany in the women's kayak four as Fanny Fischer, Nicole Reinhardt, Katrin Wagner-Augustin and Conny Wassmuth took the honours after leading for the majority of the race.

Meanwhile, US duo Philip Dalhausser and Todd Rogers kept their nerve – and the sand out of their eyes – to take gold in the men's beach volleyball title, defeating Fabio Magalhaes and Marcio Araujo of Brazil.

Lionel Messi-inspired Argentina achieved revenge over Nigeria for their 1996 defeat with a narrow victory in the Olympic football final on a blazing hot day in Beijing.

Messi, the 21-year-old Barcelona superstar, proved the pivotal influence, setting up a goal for Angel di Maria and regularly tormenting the Nigerian defence.

Di Maria's decisive 58th-minute strike earned the South Americans back-to-back gold medals following their 2004 triumph over neighbours Paraguay in Athens, and Messi could not disguise his pride.

'This group deserved gold,' he said. 'We knew coming in that we may never have this experience again. We are lucky that everything went well, and that we got what we wanted.'

Over at the pool, China had already got most of what they wanted following their domination of the diving competition, but their quest for a historic clean sweep of eight gold medals from eight events was ended in the most dramatic fashion.

Australia's Matthew Mitcham was the man who finally found a way to beat the hosts, but it took him until the very last dive of the final event. Mitcham was trailing China's Zhou Luxin by more than 30 points heading into the final

Lionel Messi celebrates with
goalscorer Angel di Maria after
Argentina's football final win over
Nigeria, and (opposite) soaks up the
atmosphere at the medal ceremony

Matthew Mitcham on his way to victory in the men's 10m platform diving, and (opposite) overcome with emotion on the podium

round of the men's 10m platform, but he produced the highest scoring dive in the history of the Olympics with his last effort to become Australia's first male Olympic gold medallist in diving since Dick Eve in 1924.

The 20-year-old from Sydney scored a whopping 112.10 with a back two-and-a-half somersault with two-and-a-half twists to pull off a stunning upset.

'It's absolutely surreal, I never thought that this would be possible,' Mitcham said. 'I wasn't even sure of my medal chances at all. After I did my last dive and I saw I was in first, I thought, "That's it, it's a silver medal, I am so happy with this", and then I won. I can't believe it, I'm so happy.

'I had some very wise words and some very good advice before coming into the 10m competition, to just enjoy it, have fun, and that's what I thought

right from the very first dive in the prelims to the very last dive in the final.

'I was definitely stressing it to myself: just enjoy the moment, there is nothing you can do to change what's about to happen, so just enjoy it, and it worked.'

There was more drama on the track as Kenenisa Bekele became the first man to complete the Olympic 5,000m and 10,000m double for 28 years. After successfully defending his 10,000m crown the week before, Bekele blew away the field to comfortably win the 5,000m in an Olympic-record time.

He said: 'This is very special for myself and also for my country. I did what I dreamed before. My plan was to pick up the pace very fast. It was a very fast race.'

Elsewhere, Britain's fine tradition in the Olympic boxing ring continued as James DeGale took middleweight gold

with a 16–14 win over Cuba's Emilio Correa Bayeux. DeGale raced into an 11–5 lead halfway through the contest and, although his opponent battled back, the Londoner was always in front and held on to secure Team GB's only boxing gold in Beijing.

Thailand's Somjit Jongjohor won the flyweight category with an 8–2 victory over Cuba's Andris Laffita Hernandez, and Felix Diaz of the Dominican Republic claimed the light-welterweight title.

Ukrainian Vasyl Lomachenko took the gold in the featherweight class after the referee stopped the fight with him leading France's Khedafi Djelkhir 9–1 after the opening round.

In the women's high jump, Blanka Vlasic's 34-competition unbeaten run came to an end as Tia Hellebaut of Belgium snatched gold, while Norway's Andreas Thorkildsen defended his javelin title in brilliant style with an Olympic record throw of 90.57m.

Kenya's Wilfred Bungei led from the front to take gold in the men's 800m final, and countrywoman Nancy Langat caused an upset in the women's 1500m as she took on pre-race favourite Maryam Yusuf Jamal down the back straight and went on to win.

There was some redemption for the United States' sprinters following their shambolic relay performances of day 13 when Sanya Richards' inspirational last leg saw them defend their women's 4x400m crown from Russia, while the men's team followed suit, finishing just outside the world record.

And in the women's cross-country mountain bike, Germany's Sabine Spitz opened up a winning margin on the first lap and held on to her advantage to take the gold. The 2003 world champion and Athens bronze medallist was so far ahead that she even had time to stop just short of the finishing line and carry her bike over her head through the

British boxer James DeGale (above) heads for middleweight gold with victory over Cuba's Emilio Correa Bayeux, while (left) another Cuban, Andris Laffita Hernandez, hits the canvas as Thailand's Somjit Jongjohor wins the flyweight final

tape. Defending Olympic champion and four-time world champion Julien Absalon of France cruised to victory in the men's event with compatriot Jean-Christophe Peraud taking silver.

Meanwhile, it was another day of drama at the Shunyi Olympic Rowing-Canoeing Park as Australia's Ken Wallace, bronze medallist in the men's 1,000m single kayak, added a gold to his collection with victory in the 500m event.

Defending champion Adam van Koeverden had to settle for silver, narrowly ahead of Briton Tim Brabants.

Reigning Olympic champions Katalin Kovacs and Natasa Janics of Hungary retained their women's flatwater K2 500m title while Russia's Maxim Opalev took gold in the men's single canoe 500m and Ukraine's Inna Osypenko-Radomska edged gold in the women's equivalent.

Germany took their first men's hockey gold since 1992 when they beat Spain 1–0, Russia won the synchronised swimming, South Korea beat Cuba to take baseball gold and China completed a 1-2-3 in the men's table tennis.

But in the volleyball it was all about Brazil as they won a first Olympic women's gold in the sport to round off a memorable day at the Games for the South Americans. ■

Quadruple world
champion Julien
Absolon heads for a
second successive
Olympic gold in the
cross-country
mountain bike event

Dwyane Wade on his way to 27 points in the basketball final

America's basketball stars saved their best until last as they finally earned redemption for their failure in Athens on the final day of action at the Games.

The pressure was on Mike Krzyzewski's talent-packed side as they went into the decisive match of the competition looking to erase the memories of four years previously, when Argentina had forced them into the bronze medal position in one of the biggest shocks in Olympic history.

There was to be no repeat upset in China, however, as the flamboyant Kobe Bryant scored 13 of his 20 points in the second half to see them safely home against Spain.

The Americans won 118–107 in the end to take the gold medal, with Dwyane Wade adding 27 points against the defending world champions. It was the perfect way for the United States to round off the Games and halt a disappointing run that had seen them falter in their last three international basketball competitions.

And there was no doubting just how important the victory was for the players themselves. Forward LeBron James, who plays his domestic basketball with the Cleveland Cavaliers in the NBA, said: 'It means everything to me. We're the

American players
clasp hands in
celebration of
basketball gold

Samuel Kamau Wanjiru of Kenya on his way to a new Olympic record in the marathon

number one team. We've been so blessed with this opportunity. It's so rewarding to see your hard work pay off. This is something I've waited for, for four years.'

Meanwhile Bryant, who plays for the LA Lakers, insisted winning a gold medal for his country was a greater feeling than winning any NBA ring.

'When you're playing for your country, there's more at stake,' he said. 'I think when you're playing for the NBA championship, you're actually playing for a brand, you're playing for whatever motivation – proving people wrong or whatever. When you put on a USA uniform, you're playing for something bigger than all that. You're representing your country, and our country is going up against the other country, trying to prove who's best. For me, that holds more weight.'

The Wukesong Indoor Stadium basketball court was the centre of most of the attention on the final day, but elsewhere, Olympic records continued to tumble right up until the closing ceremony.

Samuel Kamau Wanjiru of Kenya set a new benchmark of 2hr 6min 32sec in the men's marathon to claim the gold. The Kenyan smashed Carlos Lopes' 24-year-old record with relative ease and could not hide his delight afterwards.

He said: 'My plan was to push the limits, push my body. Now I am very happy with my pace. It feels good to make history here. It feels good to make history for Kenya and win the gold.'

At the Beijing Workers' Indoor Arena, Zou Shiming won China's first ever boxing gold medal as the favourite took the title in the light-flyweight division against Mongolia's Serdamba Purevdor. And barely had they won their first than the hosts were celebrating another success as Zhang Xiaoping then doubled the tally with an 11–7 win over Ireland's Kenny Egan in the light-heavyweight final.

Badar-Uugan Enkhbat defeated Yankiel Leon Alarcon of Cuba to give Mongolia the gold in the bantamweight category. Roberto Cammarelle of Italy stopped Zhang Zhilei of China to take the super-heavyweight title, while Russia's Alexey Tishchenko claimed lightweight gold and Kazakhstan's

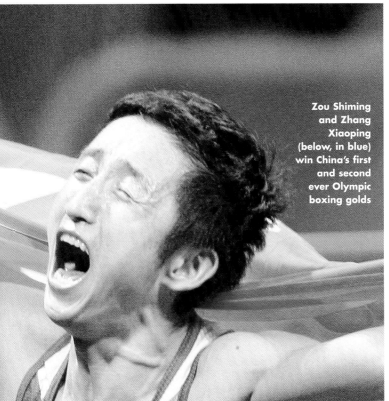

Zou Shiming and Zhang Xiaoping (below, in blue) win China's first and second ever Olympic boxing golds

Bakht Sarsekbayev beat Cuba's Carlos Banteaux Suarez 18–9 in the welterweight final.

That result ensured that the previously dominant Cuban boxing team left Beijing without a single gold – the first time the country had failed to win an Olympic boxing title since the 1968 Games in Mexico. Despite that statistic, their coach Pedro Roque refused to be too downbeat.

'The team came here with no experience, and they've won eight medals. No gold, but nobody was expecting more than one or two medals at all for us,' Roque said. 'Now we have not only eight medals, but also a team with Olympic experience ready to start preparing for the next Olympics.'

As the battle for position in the final medal table came to a dramatic climax, Russia's late surge was boosted by their women's team's performance in the group all-around final of the rhythmic gymnastics as they claimed gold ahead of hosts China.

Elsewhere, the United States won their third Olympic men's volleyball title with a 3–1 triumph over defending champions Brazil. The South Americans took the opener 25–20 before the US bounced back to take the next two sets 25–22 and 25–21. The fourth set was a thriller that swung one way and then the

other before the Americans finally edged a dramatic victory.

Earlier, Russia won its third men's volleyball medal in three consecutive Olympic Games, claiming bronze by beating Italy 25–22, 25–19, 25–23.

France took gold in the men's handball by denying Iceland 28–23, while Hungary claimed their third consecutive water polo title after seeing off the United States as the action finally drew to a close. ▪

Russia head for gold in the group all-around rhythmic gymnastics

Drums, light wheels, bouncing fluorescent men and fantastic fireworks were the order of the night in the same way they had been 16 days earlier, but that opening party now seemed like a lifetime ago.

Just like the introduction, the closing ceremony was conducted with an excitement, verve and precision that characterised the Beijing Games wherever you went. It was as if the Chinese were saying, or perhaps screaming, 'You won't forget us in a hurry!'

At the centre of everything was one final masterpiece of choreography – the Memory Tower: a writhing mass of human bodies climbing, struggling and dancing along a giant metal frame. It was a fitting tribute to the hundreds of athletes who had struggled their way to glory over the previous two weeks.

This was not the Olympics saying goodbye to Beijing; this was Beijing saying goodbye to the Olympics.

And so finally, the Olympic flame was extinguished and the Games bowed out in the inevitable blaze of fireworks.

The curtain had fallen on the 29th Olympiad of the modern era, with the baton passing to London for 2012. There was no doubt at all, however, that Beijing had made a lasting mark. ∎

It started with cycling glory in the shadow of the Great Wall of China and culminated with gold in a boxing ring in the heart of Beijing. The 2008 Games was a story of almost unprecedented success....

Great Britain's Olympians arrive home at Heathrow in a British Airways plane with a specially-painted gold nosecone

Middleweight boxer James DeGale's gold medal was Great Britain's 19th of a brilliantly successful Olympics

When middleweight boxer James DeGale crumpled to his knees in the Workers' Gymnasium after claiming gold on the penultimate evening of the Beijing 2008 Games, he sealed Great Britain's greatest Olympics for a century.

DeGale heard the national anthem ring out in the Chinese capital for the 19th time as a Games which had begun in rather inauspicious fashion for the British team evolved into a triumphant fortnight-long medal rush.

DeGale's nailbiting victory would stand alongside golds for the likes of Chris Hoy, Rebecca Adlington and Ben Ainslie as abiding images with which to equip the country for the four-year push towards London 2012.

Welsh cyclist Nicole Cooke claimed road race gold in the shadow of the Great Wall of China on the second day of the Games and the medals kept coming, not least in the velodrome, which yielded an extraordinary 12 podium finishes.

Hoy became the first Briton in 100 years to win three golds at the same Games when he added victory in the individual sprint to his earlier successes in the team sprint and the keirin.

'I was vaguely aware of the history but I tried to keep it furthest from my mind,' said Hoy afterwards. Victoria

Chris Hoy led the gold rush for Great Britain with three in the velodrome

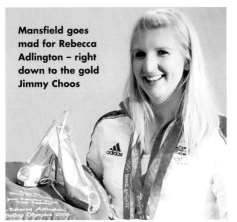

Mansfield goes mad for Rebecca Adlington – right down to the gold Jimmy Choos

Pendleton, Rebecca Romero, Bradley Wiggins and the men's team pursuit riders – including Wiggins again – also succeeded as Britain all but swept the board. Romero made history by adding her cycling medal to the silver she won as a rower in 2004.

There were also silvers for Jason Kenny, Ross Edgar, Wendy Houvenaghel and Emma Pooley, as well as bronzes for Chris Newton and Steven Burke. That was enough to delight, but far from satisfy, performance director Dave Brailsford.

'Beijing was an amazing experience,' said Brailsford, who returned home as the hottest property in the world of cycling. 'But I feel it's the start of something even better and we're determined to build on it.'

While most of the headlines in the swimming pool went to American Michael Phelps' extraordinary haul of eight gold medals, unassuming Adlington created her own significant slice of history.

The Mansfield 19-year-old swept to victory in the 400m freestyle to claim Britain's first swimming gold medal for 20 years, then followed it up by smashing a 19-year-old world record on her way to winning the 800m.

As Adlington's struck gold, her home town went into overdrive, promising her, among other things, free shoes for life and free meals in a local pub rechristened the Adlington Arms. 'I wasn't expecting this,' said Adlington on receipt of a £400 pair of Jimmy Choo shoes from the town's mayor. 'To come back with two gold medals is amazing. It's just overwhelming.'

Adlington was not the only GB swimmer to step on to the podium at the Games, with Jo Jackson taking bronze behind her in the 400m, while

Rebecca Romero (left and above centre) won a cycling gold to add to her rowing silver from the Athens Olympics in 2004

Keri-Anne Payne and Cassie Patten finished second and third respectively in the women's 10km open water marathon and David Davies took silver in the men's equivalent.

On the Shunyi lake, Britain's rowers proved once again there is plenty of life after Sir Steve Redgrave, with six medals including two golds for the men's coxless four and the men's lightweight double sculls.

World number one Tim Brabants kept the pressure at bay to storm to victory in the men's kayak 1,000m final, later also picking up a bronze in his less favoured 500m sprint. By that stage, David Florence had also already grabbed a silver medal in the men's canoe slalom single.

The nation's success on water was not confined to Beijing. In Qingdao, Britain once again dominated the Olympic regatta with Ainslie's third consecutive gold one of four claimed by the buoyant British team. There was also silver joy for Nick Rogers and Joe Glanfield and success in the windsurfing when Bryony Shaw claimed bronze. Ainslie's triumph

Team GB medal winners (left to right, from top) Nicole Cooke, Rebecca Adlington, Joanne Jackson, David Florence, Daisy Dick, William Fox-Pitt, Tina Cook, Sharon Hunt, Mary King, Emma Pooley, Jason Kenny, Jamie Staff, Chris Hoy, Tom James, Steve Williams, Pete Reed, Andrew Triggs-Hodge, Bradley Wiggins, Ross Edgar, Elise Laverick, Anna Bebington, Matthew Wells, Stephen Rowbotham, Chris Newton, Steven Burke, Sarah Ayton, Sarah Webb, Pippa Wilson, Zac Purchase, Mark Hunter, Ben Ainslie, Rebecca Romero, Annie Vernon, Debbie Flood, Frances Houghton, Katherine Grainger, Wendy Houvenaghel, Alex Partridge, Tom Stallard, Tom Lucy, Richard Egington, Josh West, Alastair Heathcote, Colin Smith, Matt Langridge, Acer Nethercott, Louis Smith, Paul Manning, Ed Clancy, Geraint Thomas, Joe Glanfield, Nick Rogers, Paul Goodison, Victoria Pendleton, Christine Ohuruogu, Jason Kenny, Germaine Mason, Keri-Anne Payne, Cassie Patten, Bryony Shaw, Natasha Danvers, David Davies, Iain Percy, Andrew Simpson, Phillips Idowu, Tim Brabants, Heather Fell, Tony Jeffries, David Price, Sarah Stevenson and James DeGale was later put into context by the president of the International Olympic Committee, Jacques Rogge, who said: 'His achievement is as valid as Phelps or [Usain] Bolt. What they do is fantastic, but what Ben Ainslie does is equally fantastic.'

Christine Ohuruogu won Britain's only track and field gold of the Games in the women's 400m but another gallant, tearful failure by Paula Radcliffe also made the headlines, as she struggled with injury and finished 23rd in the women's marathon. 'I was trying to achieve the impossible because of the amount of running I had done, but it wasn't enough,' said Radcliffe, four years after pulling out midway through her race in Athens. 'You can't take short-cuts in the marathon.'

There were, however, silver medals for Germaine Mason in the high jump and Phillips Idowu in the triple jump, while Natasha Danvers took bronze in the women's 400m hurdles.

Louis Smith became the first Briton ever to win an individual apparatus medal with bronze in the men's pommel horse, while there was a silver for Heather Fell in the modern pentathlon, and two equestrian bronzes in Hong Kong.

Sarah Stevenson won Britain's first taekwondo medal, going on to take

Ben Ainslie sails to a third successive gold medal, an achievement hailed by IOC President Jacques Rogge

Sarah Stevenson on the attack in her controversial bout with Chen Zhong

bronze after a remarkable series of events which saw her retrospectively awarded a first-round victory over Chinese favourite Chen Zhong.

Chen was initially awarded a 2–1 win but replays clearly showed Stevenson connecting with a two-point kick to the face in the final second – and officials announced an unprecedented change to the result.

Meanwhile, in the boxing ring, DeGale's gold and bronzes for David Price and Tony Jeffries ensured Britain's best performance for 56 years.

The 14-year-old synchronised diver Tom Daley had been the talk of the world's press in the run-up to the Games and, although he finished eighth with partner Blake Aldridge in the 10m event, there was plenty to build on for 2012.

However, the spirit of Great Britain's historic success in Beijing was perhaps best encapsulated by BMX rider Shanaze Reade, who paid the ultimate price for refusing to accept second best. She had silver in the bag approaching the last bend but chose to attack leader Anne Caroline Chausson, clipping her wheel and crashing out with no medal at all.

'It is the Olympics,' Reade shrugged. 'You have to give it everything and go for gold.'

Tom Daley has a philosophical shrug after finishing eighth in the synchronised diving – but he has 2012 to look forward to

Shanaze Reade
refuses to accept
second best but
crashes in her
all-or-nothing
attempt to overtake
eventual winner
Anne Caroline
Chausson in the
women's BMX final

The 2008 Olympic Games may have captured the attention of the world for two-and-a-half weeks, but some of the memories from Beijing will last forever....

Lightning Bolt strikes

'It's a wonderful day for Jamaica,' declared the country's Prime Minister Bruce Golding after Usain Bolt lowered his own world record by three hundredths of a second to become the new Olympic 100m champion and the fastest man on the planet.

Even compatriot Asafa Powell, the man tipped by many to challenge Bolt for gold in what had been billed as the 'race of the century', was left dumbfounded by what he saw in the Bird's Nest stadium. 'He was untouchable,' admitted Powell. 'He's spectacular. He's definitely the greatest.'

Phelps completes his great eight

Over the course of nine mesmerising days Michael Phelps etched his name firmly into Olympic folklore. The 23-year-old American finally eclipsed Mark Spitz's record of seven gold medals at a single Games – set in Munich in 1972 – when the Americans took victory in the men's 4x100m medley relay. Even Phelps himself seemed overawed by the achievement. 'What more could I have done?' he said.

Games over for Xiang

Home hero Liu Xiang was supposed to be the star of the Beijing 2008 Games but when an Achilles injury forced his shock withdrawal on the starting line in the opening round of the 110m hurdles, the whole of China let out a cry of despair.

The 'Shanghai Express' cut a desolate figure as he limped down the tunnel. 'The air in the stadium froze and the woman sitting next to me began to cry,' recalled Gao Xin, one of the 90,000-strong crowd. 'The Bird's Nest was in grief.'

Hoy's golden hat-trick

Cyclist Chris Hoy's hat-trick heroics ensured he became the first British athlete to claim a trio of titles at a single Olympics since swimmer Henry Taylor in 1908, when he defeated Jason Kenny in the men's sprint.

British Cycling's performance director Dave Brailsford led the tributes to Hoy, saying: 'He's a true gentleman and to me he embodies what a true Olympic athlete is meant to be.'

Clash of the superpowers

Even the appearance in the crowd of the most powerful man in the world could not divert attention as the United States and China clashed on a basketball court at the Wukesong Indoor Stadium.

American president George W Bush was among those watching as the two superpowers battled it out. The United States won but, such was the frenzy of excitement, the Chinese spectators barely seemed to notice!

Matos is no Angel

Beijing 2008 was witness to one of the more bizarre incidents in recent Olympic history when Cuba's Angel Valodia Matos kicked Swedish referee Chakir Chelbat in the face after he was disqualified from the +80kg taekwondo bronze-medal match.

Matos lashed out at Chelbat after the referee ruled he had exceeded the one-minute injury time limit and awarded the bout to Kazakhstan's Arman Chilmanov.

War ... in bikinis

Political tension between Georgia and Russia at the time ensured that when the two countries faced each other at Chaoyang Park in the beach volleyball competition there would be plenty of talking points.

And so it proved as Georgia's victory, which came courtesy of Brazilian-born duo of Christine Santanna and Andrezza Chagas, sparked an extraordinary war of words. 'They are not even Georgians,' blasted Russia's Alexandra Shiryaeva.

Adlington makes a splash

Prior to Beijing, few people outside of Mansfield had heard of Rebecca Adlington, but that all changed when the 19-year-old became Britain's most successful female swimmer with gold medals in the 400m and 800m freestyle.

In the process, Adlington broke one of swimming's most illustrious world records in the 800m, set by Janet Evans 19 years previously, to confirm her status as a new British sporting icon.

Isinbayeva poles apart

Yelena Isinbayeva had already won gold in the women's pole vault when she decided to try and break her own world record.

After a tense wait as she composed herself under a large duvet-like sheet, she did it with a leap of 5.05m at the third attempt.

Critics had questioned whether the Russian great could become a two-time Olympic gold medallist but she did so in devastating fashion. 'I wanted to prove who I am and who is the best,' she said.

Abrahamian wrestles with controversy

Swedish wrestler Ara Abrahamian hit the headlines for all the wrong reasons after a controversial ending to his semi-final bout in the men's Greco-Roman 84kg category.

Abrahamian won a bronze despite losing out to Italy's Andrea Minguzzi but, furious with what he clearly perceived as biased refereeing, he threw his medal into the middle of the wrestling ring in protest. The International Olympic Committee

was not impressed and subsequently stripped him of his award for violating the spirit of fair play.

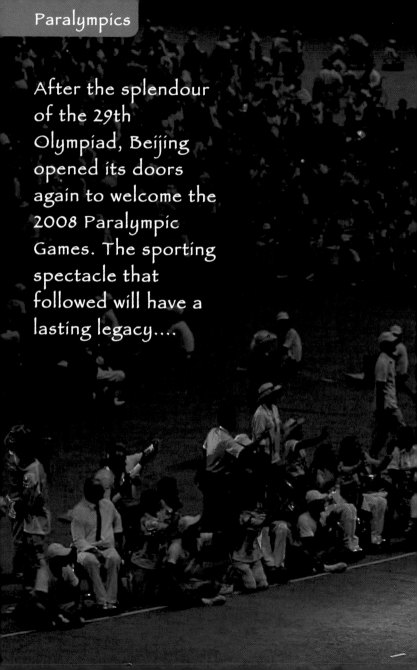

After the splendour of the 29th Olympiad, Beijing opened its doors again to welcome the 2008 Paralympic Games. The sporting spectacle that followed will have a lasting legacy....

China promised 'two Games, equal splendour' and it delivered emphatically as the 13th Paralympic Games were widely lauded as the best yet.

Just like the Olympics that had gone before, the spectacular sporting feats on show from September 6 to 17 exceeded all expectations, but the long-term effects for China of hosting the Games could be even more profound.

Prior to the 2008 Paralympics, the country's 83 million disabled – six per cent of the 1.3 billion population – were widely viewed as a marginalised section of society, yet by the time the flame was extinguished on the closing ceremony at the magnificent Bird's Nest stadium, the People's Republic of China had embraced the Games as a celebration of humanity.

The capacity crowd cheered at the top of their voices to acclaim the astonishing performances of more than 4,000 athletes from 147 countries across 20 different sports.

There was no shortage of iconic moments for them to reflect on. South African swimmer Natalie Du Toit won five gold medals in the Water Cube, Canadian wheelchair racer Chantal Petitclerc took her personal haul to 14 gold medals across five Games and South African amputee sprinter Oscar Pistorius won three titles on the track to emulate Jamaican Olympic sensation Usain Bolt.

However, they were not alone as myriad outstanding displays captured the imagination of the watching public. From goalball, where the crowd were captivated despite having to remain

**Spectators were amazed at the
ferocity of the wheelchair rugby**

silent so the visually impaired competitors could hear the bell in the ball, to boccia, a boules-like game for people with severe cerebral palsy, the spectators came in their droves to watch every single medal being won.

In wheelchair rugby the ferocity of the collisions left audiences aghast, while the sitting volleyball, where amputees worked in unison to propel the ball over the net, was another example of the unifying ability of the Games. Quite simply, the Paralympics thrilled at every turn.

As had been widely expected, China demonstrated their sporting supremacy

'It was a journey to show the indomitable spirit of mankind. I wanted to send the message to the world,' said Hou Bin after hoisting himself 40 metres from the stadium floor to light the torch at the Paralympics opening ceremony

in emphatic fashion as they blitzed the record-breaking totals recorded in Athens. They took their number of gold medals from 63 in Greece to 89 in Beijing, and from 141 to 211 in total.

Great Britain, runners-up in the medal stakes in Sydney and Athens, were the second-best nation once again. They challenged China's dominance for two thirds of the Games before the hosts accelerated away in the home straight.

The tone was set from the moment the opening ceremony began. It was a celebration of 'transcendence, integration and equality', which left the 90,000-capacity crowd in the Bird's Nest and millions of television viewers back home spellbound.

A group of the hosts' finest athletes – including Pin Yali, China's first Paralympic gold medallist – escorted the Paralympic torch on its final journey before Hou Bin, who lost his left leg at the age of nine before going on to triumph in the high jump at the last three Games, had the honour of lighting the flame.

Hou's 40-metre ascent up a rope from the stadium floor to the roof using only his arms and his willpower was the climax of the extravaganza and epitomised the Paralympic spirit.

'It was a journey to show the indomitable spirit of mankind. I wanted

Darren Kenny led Great Britain's cycling charge with four golds – three on the track and another on the road

Americans Erin Popovich (left) and Jessica Long each won four golds in the pool

to send the message to the world,' Hou said.

Hou was unable to bid for a fourth successive title as his event had been removed from the Paralympic programme due to a lack of participants, but he predicted his performance at the opening ceremony would pave the way for a change of attitude in China. 'I think the 2008 Beijing Paralympics are a historic turning point for the special group of physically challenged people who are participating or witnessing these Games,' he added. 'More and more people are getting to know us through the Paralympic Games. Actually, when you know us better, you will realise that we share the same aspirations as anyone else.'

When the action began, China soon established their dominance across the sports, although Britain and the United States challenged them on the back of strong performances in the cycling and swimming respectively. Britain won the

first three events at the Laoshan Velodrome and in four days of track cycling they collected 12 titles from 13 events entered. Australia were the second most successful cycling nation with three golds, illustrating the gulf between Britain and the rest.

It was a remarkable performance by Team GB, with Darren Kenny leading the way with three track golds before claiming a fourth on the road.

Britain's biking brilliance continued at the Ming Tombs Reservoir, with five golds from nine events entered, two better than nearest rivals the United States.

The USA were the most accomplished aquatic performers at the Games, claiming 17 gold medals – four more than China – and 44 in all. Erin Popovich and Jessica Long each won four golds and six medals in total for the Americans, but there was no doubting the real star at the Water Cube.

Du Toit stole the headlines as she successfully defended all five titles she

GB's Paralympic stars

Sarah Storey (Cycling)

Swimmer-turned-cyclist Storey was one of Britain's most decorated Paralympians as a swimmer but switched sports in 2005 when an ear infection kept her out of the water, and she has not looked back.

Storey, who is married to cycling teammate Barney Storey, made her Paralympic debut in Barcelona aged 14, winning two gold medals, three silvers and one bronze in the pool under her maiden name Bailey.

She was already no stranger to Paralympic success, but replicated her feats in the water with a gold medal at the velodrome in Beijing, winning the women's individual pursuit event in a new world record of 3min 36.637sec.

Natalie Du Toit, who also competed in the Olympics, was the joint most successful Paralympian in Beijing with five gold medals

had won in Athens. The 24-year-old, who lost her left leg in a road accident in 2001, was South Africa's flag-bearer for the Olympic and Paralympic opening ceremonies and she finished 16th in the 10km open water Olympic swimming event.

Du Toit, one of two amputees to compete in the Olympics, along with Polish table-tennis player Natalia Partyka, opened her Paralympic campaign with victory in the women's S9 100m butterfly before adding wins in the 100m freestyle, the 200m individual medley and the 400m freestyle. The major obstacle in her bid for 10 Paralympic titles was the 50m freestyle. Having endured a gruelling distance programme in preparation for the Games, she had neglected her sprint work, so it was all the more remarkable when she prevailed in the one-length dash on the final day of the swimming programme.

'I don't really train all year for the sprints,' she said. 'This was probably my toughest race and I'm just very relieved.'

Over in the Bird's Nest, it was Du Toit's compatriot Pistorius who was the most eye-catching performer. The double amputee, dubbed Blade Runner

GB's Paralympic stars

David Weir *(Athletics)*

The 29-year-old from Surrey ranks as something of a Paralympic veteran, having made his Games debut in 1996, and he added to his already extensive medal collection in Beijing.

Before competing at the 2008 Games, he won three consecutive London Marathons and three gold medals at the last World Championships in 2006. Paralympic honours had continued to elude him, however, until he claimed victory in the men's wheelchair 1,500m and 800m events in China to complete a memorable golden double on the track.

South African star Oscar Pistorius heads for gold in the T44 400m to add to his victories in the 100m and 200m

GB's Paralympic stars

Lee Pearson
(Equestrian)

Since his first Games in Sydney in 2000, Pearson has never been beaten in an equestrian event at the Paralympics.

The rider, who has a condition called arthrogryposis, which inhibits the development of muscles, rode his own bay gelding, Gentleman, at Beijing 2008 and continued his domination of the grade 1b class. His haul of three golds, and nine medals in total, made him one of Team GB's most successful competitors.

due to his prosthetic limbs, came to worldwide prominence at the age of 17 in Athens with victory in the men's T44 200m. He successfully won an appeal to compete in the 400m at the Beijing Olympics after a long legal battle, but subsequently failed to achieve the qualifying time.

Pistorius found the going difficult as he won the men's T44 400m title in wet conditions, clocking a world record of 47.49sec on the final evening of competition. That was his third gold medal, following victories in the 100m and 200m, and led to him being compared with Olympic hero Bolt, the winner of gold medals in the 100m, 200m and 4x100m relay the previous month.

Pistorius described his achievement as 'One of the proudest moments of my life. Before I came here I had a lot of goals and dreams to achieve and work towards. To achieve them and reach my goals in this competition has been amazing.'

The South African is now determined to compete in both the Paralympics and the Olympics in 2012. He continued: 'London is my next long-term goal, but first I have the World Championships in Berlin next year.'

Like Pistorius, Petitclerc was unbeatable on the track as she won all

GB's Paralympic stars

David Roberts *(Swimming)*

The Welshman's glittering career continued with another superb performance in Beijing.

The 28-year-old won four gold medals, bringing his overall Paralympic tally to 11, after winning three golds in Sydney in 2000 and four in Athens in 2004.

Roberts was selected to carry the British flag at the closing ceremony.

Chantal Petitclerc won a clean sweep of T54 100m, 200m, 400m, 800m and 1500m

five events she entered. The Canadian wheelchair racer triumphed in the women's T54 100m, 200m, 400m, 800m and 1500m for a remarkable clean sweep in a competition she believes was her toughest yet.

'They were the most rewarding, but they were the most difficult,' the 38-year-old said of her fifth, and probably her last, Games.

When the medals were counted, Petitclerc, Du Toit and Australian swimmer Matthew Cowdrey were the most successful Paralympians of the Games with five golds each, while other notable individual performances included wheelchair tennis ace Esther Vergeer, who extended her singles winning streak to 350 matches by clinching gold.

On a team level, China's all-round performance was also astounding as they claimed the status of leading nation in seven of the 20 sports.

Britain had already conceded there was no chance of overhauling the home nation prior to the Games but, come London 2012, the next hosts will be expected to challenge on all fronts, just like their predecessors. The athletics

GB's Paralympic stars

Aileen McGlynn (Cycling)

The Glasgow cyclist won four gold medals at the World Disability Championships and the Paralympic Games in Athens before moving on to her double gold triumph at the velodrome in Beijing. McGlynn was born partially sighted and races on a tandem with a pilot rider, and was partnered by Ellen Hunter in Beijing.

Swiss athlete Edith Hunkeler crashes and starts a controversial chain of events in the T54 5,000m

team will be required to lead the way if Britain are to improve on their Beijing display, although the return of two golds, both for wheelchair racer David Weir, and 17 medals in total from the track and field programme could have been improved had it not been for official interventions.

First, Shelly Woods was forced to return a silver medal presented to her following a second-place finish in the women's T54 5,000m. A crash on the penultimate lap saw more than half of the 11-athlete field sprawled across the track and the International Paralympic Committee ordered an unprecedented re-run. Canada's Diane Roy was denied gold and was subsequently beaten to silver by American Amanda McGrory in the re-run, while Woods finished third to claim bronze.

Weir, competing in his third Games having made his debut aged 17 in Atlanta, thought he had ended his 12-year wait for Paralympic glory in the men's T54 800m but a protest over a lanes mix-up left the Briton facing a re-run. In one final twist, however, the appeal was subsequently dropped and Weir finally claimed his long-awaited

GB's Paralympic stars

Eleanor Simmonds (Swimming)

Simmonds was the youngest member of the 2008 GB Paralympic team at the tender age of just 13.

The Swansea swimmer, who was born with achondroplasia, or dwarfism, got her Games off to a flying start when she won the women's 100m freestyle title, and six days later she was crowned a double Paralympic champion, and Britain's most successful female competitor, after adding the 400m title to her triumph.

gold. More medal confusion hit Britain when thrower Rebecca Chin, who had been re-classified on the eve of the Games from the 'autres' (other) F44 category to the cerebral palsy F38 category, had to return a silver medal she had won in the discus. The 16-year-old's classification was confirmed following her 10th-place finish in the shot put, but the IPC insisted Chin was 'not eligible, not matching the sport class profile' after she 'showed significantly different skill sets'.

Medal mix-ups and classification concerns aside, the theme of the 2008 Paralympic Games was overwhelmingly one of sporting brilliance. The statistics speak for themselves: a total of 279 world records were set and 339 Paralympic records broken in competition for 472 gold medals.

Such performances received the acclaim they deserved from large and appreciative crowds and the Beijing Organising Committee revealed attendances at several Paralympics venues had bettered the number of Olympic spectators, with a record 1.9 million tickets sold.

Just as at the Olympics, for nearly two weeks the attention of the world focused on Beijing. China delivered a Paralympic Games that no one will ever forget. ■

Athletes parade for the closing ceremony in the Bird's Nest stadium

Games by numbers

19
gold medals won by Team GB – the most since 1908

47
medals won by Team GB

2,286
the number of medals won by the United States in Olympic history, comprising 926 gold, 725 silver and 635 bronze and putting them top of the all-time medal table

87
nations won medals in Beijing

91,000
seats in the Bird's Nest Stadium

707
the number of medals won by Great Britain in Olympic history, comprising 204 gold, 254 silver and 249 bronze and leaving them third in the all-time medal table

302
events

£250m
cost of the Bird's Nest Stadium

37
venues

25
world swimming records set in the Water Cube

10,500
athletes

300
hours of TV coverage on BBC1 and BBC2

19.3
the new world record, in seconds, set by Usain Bolt in the 200m final

20,000
media

204
nations took part

9.69
the new world record, in seconds, set by Usain Bolt in the 100m final

4
countries won medals for the first time – Afghanistan, Togo, Tajikistan and Mauritius

500,000
volunteers

Games by numbers

8:14.1 the new world record, in minutes and seconds, set by Rebecca Adlington in the 800m freestyle final

132 Olympic records set

8 said to be China's lucky number. The Games started at 8pm on 08/08/08

110 medals won by the US – more than any other country

14 years 80 days the age of British diver Tom Daly at the start of the Games

8 gold medals won by Michael Phelps

3:53.314 the world record in the men's team pursuit final, in minutes and seconds, set by GB's Ed Clancy, Paul Manning, Geraint Thomas and Bradley Wiggins, beating their previous world record of 3:55.202 set in the first round

103 the age of Fu Yiquan, the oldest Games volunteer

33,000 meals were served every day in the Olympic Village, by 2,400 kitchen staff

67 the age of the oldest participant, dressage rider Hiroshi Hoketsu

43 world records set

37.1 the new world record, in seconds, set in the 4x100m final by Michael Frater, Asafa Powell, Usain Bolt and Nesta Carter of Jamaica

28 sports

5 countries won a single bronze medal

27/7/2012 date of the opening ceremony of the London Games

Games by numbers

Final Olympic medal table 2008

	G	S	B	Total		G	S	B	Total
China	51	21	28	100	Latvia	1	1	1	3
United States	36	38	36	110	Belgium	1	1	0	2
Russia	23	21	28	72	Dominican Republic	1	1	0	2
Great Britain	19	13	15	47	Estonia	1	1	0	2
Germany	16	10	15	41	Portugal	1	1	0	2
Australia	14	15	17	46	India	1	0	2	3
Korea	13	10	8	31	Iran	1	0	1	2
Japan	9	6	10	25	Bahrain	1	0	0	1
Italy	8	10	10	28	Cameroon	1	0	0	1
France	7	16	17	40	Panama	1	0	0	1
Ukraine	7	5	15	27	Tunisia	1	0	0	1
Netherlands	7	5	4	16	Sweden	0	4	1	5
Jamaica	6	3	2	11	Croatia	0	2	3	5
Spain	5	10	3	18	Lithuania	0	2	3	5
Kenya	5	5	4	14	Greece	0	2	2	4
Belarus	4	5	10	19	Trinidad & Tobago	0	2	0	2
Romania	4	1	3	8	Nigeria	0	1	3	4
Ethiopia	4	1	2	7	Austria	0	1	2	3
Canada	3	9	6	18	Ireland	0	1	2	3
Poland	3	6	1	10	Serbia	0	1	2	3
Hungary	3	5	2	10	Algeria	0	1	1	2
Norway	3	5	2	10	Bahamas	0	1	1	2
Brazil	3	4	8	15	Columbia	0	1	1	2
Czech Republic	3	3	0	6	Kyrgyzstan	0	1	1	2
Slovakia	3	2	1	6	Morocco	0	1	1	2
New Zealand	3	1	5	9	Tajikistan	0	1	1	2
Georgia	3	0	3	6	Chile	0	1	0	1
Cuba	2	11	11	24	Ecuador	0	1	0	1
Kazakhstan	2	4	7	13	Iceland	0	1	0	1
Denmark	2	2	3	7	Malaysia	0	1	0	1
Mongolia	2	2	0	4	South Africa	0	1	0	1
Thailand	2	2	0	4	Singapore	0	1	0	1
DPR Korea	2	1	3	6	Sudan	0	1	0	1
Argentina	2	0	4	6	Vietnam	0	1	0	1
Switzerland	2	0	4	6	Armenia	0	0	6	6
Mexico	2	0	1	3	Chinese Taipei	0	0	4	4
Turkey	1	4	3	8	Afghanistan	0	0	1	1
Zimbabwe	1	3	0	4	Egypt	0	0	1	1
Azerbaijan	1	2	4	7	Israel	0	0	1	1
Uzbekistan	1	2	3	6	Rep. of Moldova	0	0	1	1
Slovenia	1	2	2	5	Mauritius	0	0	1	1
Bulgaria	1	1	3	5	Togo	0	0	1	1
Indonesia	1	1	3	5	Venezuela	0	0	1	1
Finland	1	1	2	4					

Final Paralympic medal table 2008

	G	S	B	Total
China	89	70	52	211
Great Britain	42	29	31	102
United States	36	35	28	99
Ukraine	24	18	32	74
Australia	23	29	27	79
South Africa	21	3	6	30
Canada	19	10	21	50
Russian Fed.	18	23	22	63
Brazil	16	14	17	47
Spain	15	21	22	58
Germany	14	25	20	59
France	12	21	19	52
Korea	10	8	13	31
Mexico	10	3	7	20
Tunisia	9	9	3	21
Czech Republic	6	3	18	27
Japan	5	14	8	27
Poland	5	12	13	30
Netherlands	5	10	7	22
Greece	5	9	10	24
Belarus	5	7	1	13
Iran	5	6	3	14
Cuba	5	3	6	14
New Zealand	5	3	4	12
Sweden	5	3	4	12
Hong Kong, China	5	3	3	11
Kenya	5	3	1	9
Italy	4	7	7	15
Egypt	4	4	4	12
Nigeria	4	4	1	9
Algeria	4	3	8	15
Morocco	4	1	2	7
Austria	4	1	1	6
Switzerland	3	2	6	11
Denmark	3	2	4	9
Ireland	3	1	1	5
Croatia	3	1	0	4
Azerbaijan	2	3	5	10
Slovakia	2	3	1	6
Finland	2	2	2	6
Thailand	1	5	7	13
Portugal	1	4	2	7
Norway	1	3	3	7
Cyprus	1	2	1	4
Latvia	1	2	0	3
Singapore	1	1	2	4
Venezuela	1	1	2	4
Saudi Arabia	1	1	0	2
Hungary	1	0	5	6
Chinese Taipei	1	0	1	2
Turkey	1	0	1	2
Mongolia	1	0	0	1
Israel	0	5	1	6
Angola	0	3	0	3
Jordan	0	2	2	4
Lithuania	0	2	0	2
Serbia	0	2	0	2
Argentina	0	1	5	6
Slovenia	0	1	2	3
Bulgaria	0	1	1	2
Colombia	0	1	1	2
Iraq	0	1	1	2
Bosnia/Herzegov	0	1	0	1
Pakistan	0	1	0	1
Papua N Guinea	0	1	0	1
Romania	0	1	0	1
UA Emirates	0	1	0	1
Lebanon	0	0	2	2
Belgium	0	0	1	1
Estonia	0	0	1	1
Jamaica	0	0	1	1
Lao PDR	0	0	1	1
Malaysia	0	0	1	1
Namibia	0	0	1	1
Puerto Rico	0	0	1	1
Syrian AR	0	0	1	1

Team GB Olympic medal winners 2008

	GOLD	SILVER	BRONZE
Day 2	**Nicole Cooke** Women's cycling road race		
Day 3	**Rebecca Adlington** Women's swimming 400m freestyle		**Joanne Jackson** Women's swimming 400m freestyle
Day 4		**David Florence** Men's canoe C1 slalom	**Team equestrian eventing** (Daisy Dick, William Fox-Pitt, Sharon Hunt, Mary King, Tina Cook) **Tina Cook** Individual equestrian eventing
Day 5		**Emma Pooley** Women's road cycling individual time trial	
Day 7	**Men's track cycling team sprint** (Chris Hoy, Jason Kenny, Jamie Staff)		
Day 8	**Rebecca Adlington** Women's swimming 800m freestyle **Men's rowing four** (Tom James, Steve Williams, Pete Reed, Andy Triggs-Hodge) **Chris Hoy** Men's track cycling keirin **Bradley Wiggins** Men's track cycling individual pursuit	**Ross Edgar** Men's track cycling keirin	**Women's rowing double sculls** (Elise Laverick, Anna Bebington) **Men's rowing double sculls** (Matthew Wells, Stephen Rowbotham) **Chris Newton** Men's track cycling points race **Steven Burke** Men's track cycling individual pursuit
Day 9	**Men's rowing lightweight double sculls** (Zac Purchase, Mark Hunter) **Ben Ainslie** Men's sailing Finn **Rebecca Romero** Women's track cycling individual pursuit **Women's sailing Yngling** (Sarah Ayton, Sarah Webb, Pippa Wilson)	**Men's rowing eight** (Alex Partridge, Tom Stallard, Tom Lucy, Richard Egington, Josh West, Alastair Heathcote, Matt Langridge, Colin Smith, cox Acer Nethercott) **Women's rowing quadruple sculls** (Annie Vernon, Debbie Flood, Frances Houghton, Katherine Grainger) **Wendy Houvenaghel** Track cycling individual pursuit	**Louis Smith** Men's gymnastics pommel horse
Day 10	**Men's track cycling team pursuit** (Paul Manning, Bradley Wiggins, Ed Clancy, Geraint Thomas)	**Men's sailing 470** (Joe Glanfield, Nick Rogers)	
Day 11	**Paul Goodison** Men's sailing Laser **Victoria Pendleton** Women's track cycling individual sprint **Chris Hoy** Men's track cycling individual sprint **Christine Ohuruogu** Women's athletics 400m	**Jason Kenny** Track cycling individual sprint **Germaine Mason** Men's athletics high jump	
Day 12		**Keri-Anne Payne** Women's swimming open water 10km marathon	**Cassie Patten** Open water 10km **Bryony Shaw** RS:X windsurfing **Natasha Danvers** 400m hurdles
Day 13	**Men's sailing Star** (Iain Percy, Andrew Simpson)	**David Davies** Men's swimming open water 10km **Phillips Idowu** Men's athletics triple jump	
Day 14	**Tim Brabants** Men's kayak K1 1000m	**Heather Fell** Modern pentathlon	**Tony Jeffries** Boxing light-heavy **David Price** Boxing super-heavy
Day 15	**James DeGale** Boxing middleweight		**Tim Brabants** Kayak K1 500m **Sarah Stevenson** Taekwondo +67kg

Team GB Paralympic medal winners 2008

GOLD

Tom Aggar Men's rowing singles sculls A
Mark Bristow Men's track cycling 1km time trial LC 1
Danielle Brown Women's archery individual compound open
Sophie Christiansen Individual equestrian freestyle test grade Ia
Jody Cundy Men's track cycling 1km time trial LC 2
Anne Dunham Individual equestrian championship test grade Ia
Heather Frederiksen Women's swimming 100m backstroke S8
Sam Hynd Men's swimming 400m freestyle S8
Elizabeth Johnson Women's swimming 100m breaststroke SB6
Darren Kenny Men's cycling individual road race LC 3/LC 4/CP3
Darren Kenny Men's track cycling 1km time trial CP 3
Darren Kenny Men's track cycling individual pursuit CP 3
Sascha Kindred Men's swimming 100m breaststroke SB7
Sascha Kindred Men's swimming 200m individual medley SM6
Rachel Morris Women's road cycling individual time trial HC A/HC B/HC C
Peter Norfolk Wheelchair tennis quad singles open
Lee Pearson Individual equestrian championship test grade Ib
Lee Pearson Individual equestrian freestyle test grade Ib
Helene Raynsford Women's rowing single sculls A
Simon Richardson Men's track cycling individual pursuit LC 3
Simon Richardson Men's track cycling 1km time trial LC 3-4
David Roberts Men's swimming 50m freestyle S7
David Roberts Men's swimming 100m freestyle S7
David Roberts Men's swimming 400m freestyle S7
Eleanor Simmonds Women's swimming 100m freestyle S6
Eleanor Simmonds Women's swimming 400m freestyle S6
Matt Skelhon Mixed shooting R3-10m air rifle prone SH1
David Stone Mixed cycling individual road race CP 1/CP 2
David Stone Mixed cycling individual time trial CP 1/CP 2
Sarah Storey Women's road cycling individual time trial LC 1/LC 2/CP 4
Sarah Storey Women's track cycling individual pursuit LC 1-2/CP 4
John Stubbs Men's archery individual compound open
David Weir Men's athletics 800m T54
David Weir Men's athletics 1500m T54
Boccia mixed team BC1-2 (Dan Bentley, Nigel Murray, Zoe Robinson, David Smith)
Men's swimming 4x100m freestyle relay 34pts (Matt Walker, Graham Edmunds, David Roberts, Robert Welbourn)
Men's track cycling sprint B&VI 1-3 (Anthony Kappes, Barney Storey)
Men's track cycling team sprint LC1-4 CP3/4 (Darren Kenny, Mark Bristow, Jody Cundy)
Men's track cycling 1km time trial B&VI (Anthony Kappes, Barney Storey)
Team equestrian (Sophie Christiansen, Anne Dunham, Simon Laurens, Lee Pearson)
Women's track cycling individual pursuit B&VI 1-3 (Aileen McGlynn, Ellen Hunter)
Women's track cycling 1km time trial B&VI 1-3 (Aileen McGlynn, Ellen Hunter)

SILVER

Jim Anderson Men's swimming 50m backstroke S2
Jim Anderson Men's swimming 200m freestyle S2
Ricky Balshaw Individual equestrian freestyle test grade Ib
Mickey Bushell Men's athletics 100m T53
John Cavanagh Men's archery individual compound W1
Sophie Christiansen Individual equestrian championship test grade Ia
Libby Clegg Women's athletics 100m T12
Felicity Coulthard Individual equestrian freestyle test grade II
Gareth Duke Men's swimming 100m breaststroke SB6
Anne Dunham Individual equestrian freestyle test grade Ia
Jon Fox Men's swimming 100m backstroke S7
Heather Frederiksen Women's swimming 100m freestyle S8
Heather Frederiksen Women's swimming 400m freestyle S8
Darren Kenny Men's road cycling individual time trial CP3
Simon Laurens Individual equestrian freestyle test grade III
Nyree Lewis Women's swimming 100m backstroke S6
Chris Martin Men's athletics discus throw F33/34/52
Stephen Miller Men's athletics club throw F32/51
Nigel Murray Boccia mixed individual BC2
Simon Richardson Men's road cycling individual time trial LC3
Ben Rushgrove Men's athletics 100m T36
Rik Waddon Men's track cycling 1km time trial CP3
Matt Walker Men's swimming 50m freestyle S7
Matt Walker Men's swimming 50m butterfly S7
Louise Watkin Women's swimming 100m freestyle S9
David Weir Men's athletics 400m T54
Robert Welbourn Men's swimming 400m freestyle S10
Fran Williamson Women's swimming 50m backstroke S3
Shelly Woods Women's athletics 1500m T54

BRONZE

Jim Anderson Men's swimming 50m freestyle S2
Jim Anderson Men's swimming 100m freestyle S2
Claire Cashmore Women's swimming 100m breaststroke SB8
Mel Clarke Women's archery individual compound open
Sean Fraser Men's swimming 100m backstroke S8
Heather Frederiksen Women's swimming 200m individual medley SM8
Daniel Greaves Men's athletics discus throw F44
Sam Hynd Men's swimming 200m individual medley SM8
Samuel Ingram Men's judo -90kg
Ian Jones Men's athletics 200m T44
Ian Jones Men's athletics 400m T44
Natalie Jones Women's swimming 50m freestyle S6
Natalie Jones Women's swimming 200m individual medley SM6
Sascha Kindred Men's swimming 50m butterfly S6
John McFall Men's athletics 100m T42
Hazel Simpson Women's athletics 100m T36
Hazel Simpson Women's athletics 200m T36
Anthony Stephens Men's swimming 200m freestyle S5
Matt Walker Men's swimming 100m freestyle S7
Matt Walker Men's swimming 200m individual medley SM7
Louise Watkin Women's swimming 50m freestyle S9
Louise Watkin Women's swimming 100m breaststroke SB9
Louise Watkin Women's swimming 200m individual medley SM9
David Weir Men's athletics 5000m T54
Matt Whorwood Men's swimming 100m breaststroke SB6
Matt Whorwood Men's swimming 400m freestyle S6
Fran Williamson Women's swimming freestyle S3
Shelley Woods Women's athletics 5000m T54
Mixed rowing coxed four LTA (Victoria Hansford, Naomi Riches, Ali McKean, James Morgan, cox Alan Sherman)
Wheelchair basketball men (Simon Munn, Matthew Byrne, Ade Orogbemi, Kevin Hayes, Jon Pollock, Terence Bywater, Peter Finbow, Joseph Bestwick, Abdillah Jama, Simon Brown, Jonathan Hall, Andrew Blake)
Wheelchair tennis quad doubles open (Jamie Burdekin, Peter Norfolk)

Games by numbers

World records set at the 2008 Olympic Games

Katerina Emmons (Cze) Women's shooting 10m air rifle: 400pts (Equals WR)

Michael Phelps (USA) Men's swimming 400m individual medley: 4min 03.840sec

Men's swimming 200m freestyle: 1min 42.960sec

Men's swimming 200m individual medley: 1min 54.230sec

Men's swimming 200m butterfly: 1min 52.030sec

Stephanie Rice (Aus) Women's swimming 400m individual medley: 4min 29.450sec

Women's swimming 200m individual medley: 2min 08.450sec

Sung-Hyun Park, Ok-Hee Yun & Hyun Jung Joo (Kor)

Women's archery team: 231pts

Jason Lezak, Michael Phelps, Garrett Weber-Gale & Cullen Jones (USA)

Men's swimming 4x100m freestyle relay: 3min 08.240sec

Kirsty Coventry (Zim) Women's swimming 100m backstroke: 58.770sec

Women's swimming 200m backstroke: 2min 05.240sec

Kosuke Kitajima (Jpn) Men's swimming 100m breaststroke: 58.910sec

Federica Pellegrini (Ita) Women's swimming 200m freestyle: 1min 54.820sec

Aaron Peirsol (USA) Men's swimming 100m backstroke: 52.540sec

Eamon Sullivan (Aus) Men's swimming 100m freestyle: 47.050sec

Ryan Lochte, Michael Phelps, Peter Vanderkaay & Ricky Berens (USA)

Men's swimming 4x200m freestyle relay: 6min 58.560sec

Zige Liu (Chn) Women's swimming 200m butterfly: 2min 04.180sec

Linda Mackenzie, Stephanie Rice, Bronte Barratt & Kylie Palmer (Aus)

Women's swimming 4x200m freestyle relay: 7min 44.310sec

Rebecca Soni (USA) Women's swimming 200m breaststroke: 2min 20.220sec

Ryan Lochte (USA) Men's swimming 200m backstroke: 1min 53.940sec

Andrei Rybakou (Bel) Men's weightlifting 85kg: 394kg

Rebecca Adlington (GBR) Women's swimming 800m freestyle: 8min 14.100sec

Miran Jang (Kor) Women's weightlifting +75kg: 326kg

Usain Bolt (Jam) Men's athletics 100m: 9.69sec

Men's athletics 200m: 19.30sec

Leisel Jones, Jessicah Schipper, Emily Seebohm & Lisbeth Trickett (Aus)

Women's swimming 4x100m medley relay: 3min 52.690sec

Brendan Hansen, Jason Lezak, Michael Phelps & Aaron Peirsol (USA)

Men's swimming 4x100m medley relay: 3min 29.340sec

Ed Clancy, Paul Manning, Geraint Thomas & Bradley Wiggins (GBR)

Men's track cycling team pursuit: 03min 53.314sec

Gulnara Galkina-Samitova (Rus) Women's athletics 3000m steeplechase: 8min 58.81sec

Andrei Aramnau (Bel) Men's weightlifting 105kg: 436kg

Yelena Isinbayeva (Rus) Women's athletics pole vault: 5.05m

Michael Frater, Asafa Powell, Usain Bolt & Nesta Carter (Jam)

Men's athletics 4x100m relay: 37.10sec

World records set at the 2008 Paralympic Games

Dzmitry Salei (Bel) – Men's swimming 100m butterfly S13: 58.89sec

Patricia Valle (Mex) – Women's swimming 100m freestyle S4: 2min 02.50sec; Women's swimming 150m IM SM4: 3min 29.36sec

Darren Kenny (GBR) – Men's track cycling individual pursuit CP3: 3min 36.875sec; Men's track cycling 1km time trial CP3: 1min 08.668sec

Rudy Garcia Tolson (USA) – Men's swimming 200m individual medley SM7: 2min 35.92sec

Peter Leek (Aus) – Men's swimming 100m butterfly S8: 1min 00.95sec; Men's swimming 200m IM SM8: 2min 20.92sec

Amanda Everlove (USA) – Women's swimming 100m butterfly S8: 1min 11.64sec

Tamas Sors (Hun) – Men's swimming 100m butterfly S9: 59.34sec

Kieran Modra & Lawrence Tyson (Aus) – Men's track cycling individual pursuit B&VI 1-3: 4min 18.166sec

Valeriry Ponomarenko (Rus) – Men's shooting P1-10m air pistol SH1: 672.4pts

Simon Richardson (GBR) – Men's track cycling 1km time trial LC 3-4: 1min 14.936sec; Men's track cycling individual pursuit LC3: 3min 48.178secs

Ellen Hunter & Aileen McGlynn (GBR) – Women's track cycling 1km time trial B&VI 1-3: 1min 09.066sec

Dimitry Kokarev (Rus) – Men's swimming 200m freestyle S2: 4min 45.43sec; Men's swimming 50m backstroke S2: 1min 03.17sec

Jianping Du (Chn) – Men's swimming 100m freestyle S3: 1min 35.21sec; Men's swimming 50m backstroke S3: 44.31sec; Men's swimming 50m backstroke S3: 49.01sec

Daniel Dias (Bra) – Men's swimming 100m Freestyle S5: 1min 11.05sec; Men's swimming 200m freestyle S5: 2min 32.32sec; Men's swimming 200m IM SM5 2min 52.60sec

Maria Teresa Perales (Spa) – Women's swimming 100m freestyle S5 1min 16.65sec; Women's swimming 50m freestyle S5 35.88sec

Sascha Kindred (GBR) – Men's swimming 200m individual medley SM6: 2min 42.19sec; Men's swimming 100m breaststroke SB7: 1min 22.18sec

Miranda Uhl (USA) – Women's swimming 200m individual medley SM6: 3min 13.05sec

Erin Popovich (USA) – Women's swimming 200m individual medley SM7: 2min 54.61sec; Women's swimming 100m breaststroke SB7: 1min 31.60sec

Natalie du Toit (RSA) – Women's swimming 100m butterfly S9: 1min 06.74sec; Women's swimming 200m individual medley SM9: 2min 27.83sec; Women's swimming 400m freestyle S9: 4min 23.81sec

Elodie Lorandi (Fra) – Women's swimming 100m multiple S10: 59.80sec

Anna Efimenko (Rus) – Women's swimming 400m freestyle S13: 4min 37.37sec

Juan Reyes (Mex) – Women's swimming 50m backstroke S4: 42.71sec

Junguan He (Chn) – Men's swimming 50m backstroke S5: 35.04sec

Maksymn Veraksa (Ukr) – Men's swimming 100m Breaststroke SB12: 1min 07.46sec; Men's swimming 200m individual medley SM12: 2min 12.71sec; Men's swimming 100m freestyle S12: 51.93sec; Men's swimming 50m freestyle S12: 23.43sec

Karolina Pelendritou (Cyp) – Women's swimming 100m breaststroke SB12: 1min 16.82sec

Jonas Jacobsson (Swe) – Men's shooting R1-10m air rifle standing SH1: 596pts; Men's shooting R7-50m free rifle 3x40-SH1: 1163pts; Men's shooting R7-50m free rifle 3x40-SH1: 1264.3pts

Osamah Alshnaqiti (KSA) – Men's athletics triple jump F12: 15.37m

Andrea Hengen (Ger) – Women's athletics javelin throw F42-46: 39.23m

Jennifer Schuble (USA) – Women's track cycling 500m time trial LC1-2/CP4: 40.278sec; Women's track cycling individual pursuit LC1-2/CP4: 4min 01.243sec

Eva Kacanu (Cze) – Women's athletics shot put F54-56: 6.73m

Leonardo Diaz (Cub) – Men's athletics discus throw F55/56: 40.87m

Paula Tesoriero (NZL) – Women's track cycling 500m time trial LC3-4/CP3: 43.281sec

Anthony Kappes & Barney Storey (GBR) – Men's track cycling 1km time trial B&VI: 1min 02.864sec

Andre Brasil (Bra) – Men's swimming 100m butterfly S10: 56.47sec; Men's swimming 100m freestyle S10: 51.38sec; Men's swimming 50m freestyle S10: 23.61sec; Men's swimming 50m freestyle S10: 24.55sec

Anders Olsson (Swe) – Men's swimming 100m freestyle S6: 1min 05.95sec; Men's swimming 400m freestyle S6: 4min 48.31sec

Lixin Zhang, Huzhao Li, Ji Zhao & Kai Zong (Chn) – Men's athletics 4x100m relay T53/T54: 49.890sec

Charl Bouwer (RSA) – Men's swimming 400m freestyle S13: 4min 14.02sec

Valerie Grand Maison (Can) – Women's swimming 400m freestyle S13: 4min 28.64sec; Women's swimming 100m freestyle S13: 58.87sec

Lucas Prado (Bra) – Men's athletics 100m T11: 11.190sec; Men's athletics 100m T11: 11.030sec; Men's athletics 200m T11: 22.480sec

Christine Wolf (Aus) – Women's athletics long jump F42: 3.37m

Karim Betina (Alg) – Men's athletics shot put F32: 10.65m

Jackie Christiansen (Den) – Men's athletics shot put F44: 17.89m

Aigars Apinis (Lat) – Men's athletics discus throw F33/34/52: 20.47m; Men's athletics shot put F33/34/52: 11.05m

Matthew Cowdrey (Aus) – Men's swimming 100m freestyle S9: 55.30sec;

Men's swimming 200m individual medley SM9: 2min 13.60sec; Men's swimming 100m backstroke S9: 1min 03.34sec; Men's swimming 50m S9: 25.34sec

Wei Guo (Chn) – Men's athletics javelin throw F35/36: 56.07m; Men's athletics discus throw F35/36: 54.13m; Men's athletics shot put F35/36: 16.22m

Pawel Piotrowski (Pol) – Men's athletics javelin throw F35/36: 42.88m; Men's athletics shot put F35/36: 13.03m

Katarzyna Pawlik (Pol) – Women's swimming 100m freestyle S10: 1min 01.60sec; Women's swimming 400m freestyle S10: 4min 33.15sec

Ashley Owens (USA) – Women's swimming 100m freestyle S10: 1min 01.57sec

Paolo Vigano (Ita) – Men's track cycling individual pursuit LC4: 3min 59.741sec

Qing Wu (Chn) – Women's athletics discus throw F35/36: 25.80m; Women's athletics javelin throw F35-38: 28.84m

Inna Dyachenko (Ukr) – Women's athletics 100m T38: 13.430sec; Women's athletics 100m T38: 13.560sec; Women's athletics 200m T38: 27.810sec

Yun-Ri Lee (Kor) – Women's shooting R8-50m sport rifle 3x20-SH1: 579pts; Women's shooting R8-50m sport rifle 3x20-SH1: 676.9pts

John Stubbs (GBR) – Men's archery individual compound: 691pts

Danielle Brown (GBR) – Women's archery Individual compound: 676pts

Yanhong Xiao (Chn) – Women's archery individual recurve W1/W2: 611pts

Yanhong Xiao & Hongzhi Fu (Chn) – Women's archery individual recurve W1/W2: 1804pts

Hwa-Sook Lee (Kor) – Women's archery individual recurve: 614pts

Maria Buggenhagen (Ger) – Women's athletics discus throw F54-56: 27.80m

Alexey Ashapatov (Rus) – Men's athletics shot put F57/58: 16.03m; Men's athletics discus throw F57/58: 57.61m

Jamil Elshebli (Jor) – Men's athletics shot put F57/58: 14.28m

Masashi Ishii (Jpn) – Men's track cycling 1km time trial CP4: 1min 08.771sec

Ho-Guoung You (Kor) – Mixed shooting R5-10m air rifle prone SH2: 600pts

Viktoria Wedin (Swe) – Women's shooting R5-10m air rifle prone SH2: 600pts

Ji-Seok Lee (Kor) – Mixed shooting R5-10m air rifle prone SH2: 600pts; Mixed shooting R4-10m air rifle stand SH2: 600pts

Mark Bristow (GBR) – Men's track cycling 1km time trial LC1: 1min 08.873sec

Hong-Kyiu & Hong-Gu Lee (Kor) – Men's archery individual recurve W1/W2: 1886pts

Jody Cundy (GBR) – Men's track cycling 1km time trial LC2: 1min 05.466sec

Enhamed Enhamed (Spa) – Men's swimming 100m butterfly S11: 1min 01.12sec; Men's swimming 50m freestyle S11: 25.82sec

CONTINUED OVERLEAF

World records set at the 2008 Paralympic Games (continued)

Raman Makarau (Bel) – Men's swimming 100m butterfly S12: 56.90sec

Dmytro Vynohradets (Ukr) – Men's swimming 200m freestyle S3: 3min 22.98sec; Men's swimming 50m freestyle S3: 42.60sec

Francis Heath (Aus) – Men's swimming 200m freestyle S3: 21.740sec; Men's swimming 400m T46: 47.690sec

Richard Oribe (Spa) – Men's swimming 200m freestyle S4: 2min 55.81sec

Assia El'Hannouni (Fra) – Women's athletics 800m T13/12: 2min 04.960sec; Women's athletics 1500m T13: 4min 19.200sec; Women's athletics 200m T12: 24.840sec

Michaela Floeth (Ger) – Women's athletics shot put F42-46: 12.58m

Baozhu Zheng (Chn) – Women's athletics shot put F42-46: 10.06m

Eucharia Njideka (Ngr) – Women's athletics shot put F57/58: 10.96m

Nadia Medjemedj (Alg) – Women's athletics shot put F57/58: 10.93m

Andriy Kalyna (Ukr) – Men's swimming 100m breaststroke SB8: 1min 07.01sec

Haider Ali (Pak) – Men's athletics long jump F37/38: 6.44m (Equals WR)

Farhat Chida (Tun) – Men's athletics long jump F37/38: 6.44m

Yuxi Ma (Chn) – Men's athletics long jump F37/38: 6.19m

Olesya Vladykina (Rus) – Women's swimming 100m breaststroke SB8: 1min 20.58sec

Pieter Gruijters (Ned) – Men's athletics javelin throw F55/56: 42.27m

Dong Xia (Chn) – Men's athletics javelin throw F37/38: 57.81m; Men's athletics shot put F37/38: 16.60m

Ruel Ishaku (Ngr) – Powerlifting men's -48kg: 169kg

Lidiya Solovyova (Ukr) – Powerlifting women's -40kg: 105.5kg

Kevin Paul (RSA) – Men's swimming 100m breaststroke SB9: 1min 08.58sec; Men's swimming 100m breaststroke SB9: 1min 08.70sec

Lantz Lamback (USA) – Men's swimming 100m backstroke S7: 1min 14.06sec; Men's swimming 100m backstroke S7: 1min 12.09sec

Katrina Porter (Aus) – Women's swimming 100m backstroke S7: 1min 24.30sec; Women's swimming 100m backstroke S7: 1min 24.30sec

Konstantin Lisenkov (Rus) – Men's swimming 100m backstroke S8: 1min 06.33sec; Men's swimming 100m backstroke S8: 1min 06.72sec

Heather Frederiksen (GBR) – Women's swimming 100m backstroke S8: 1min 16.74sec; Women's swimming 100m backstroke S8: 1min 17.62sec

Natalie Simanowski (Ger) – Women's track cycling individual pursuit LC3-4/CP3: 4min 16.176sec

Barbara Buchan (USA) – Women's track cycling individual pursuit LC3-4/CP3: 4min 31.334sec

Sarah Storey (GBR) – Women's track cycling individual pursuit LC1-2/CP4: 3min 40.492sec; Women's track cycling individual pursuit LC1-2/CP4: 3min 36.637sec

Andrey Lebedinskiy (Rus) – Mixed shooting P3-25m sport pistol-SH1: 774.7pts

Charalampos Taiganidis (Gre) – Men's swimming 100m freestyle S13: 53.37sec; Men's swimming 100m backstroke S13: 59.85sec

Yunidis Castillo (Cub) – Women's athletics 100m T46: 12.040sec; Women's athletics 200m T46: 24.720sec

Jessica Galli (USA) – Women's athletics 400m T53: 54.880sec

Pengkai Zhu (Chn) – Men's athletics javelin throw F11/12: 63.07m

Abraham Cheruiyot Tarbei (Ken) – Men's athletics 1500m T46: 3min 52.500sec; Men's athletics 5000m T46: 14min 20.880sec

Roy Perkins (USA) – Men's swimming 50m butterfly S5: 35.95sec

Matt Walker, Robert Welbourn, David Roberts & Graham Edmunds (GBR) – Men's swimming 4x100m free 34pts: 3min 51.43sec

Arnaud Assoumani (Fra) – Men's athletics long jump F46: 7.23m

Roman Pavlyk (Ukr) – Men's athletics 400m T36: 54.130sec

Tetyana Yakybchuk (Ukr) – Women's athletics discus F32-34/51-53: 17.05m

Frances Herrmann (Ger) – Women's athletics discus F32/51-53: 21.19m

Michael McKillop (Ire) – Men's athletics 800m T37: 1min 59.390sec

Abderrahim Zhiou (Tun) – Men's athletics 800m T12: 1min 52.130sec

Renata Chilewska (Pol) – Women's athletics javelin throw F35-38: 25.59m

Shirlene Coelho (Bra) – Women's athletics javelin throw F35-38: 35.95m

Lixin Zhang (Chn) – Men's athletics 400m T54: 45.070sec; Men's athletics 200m T54: 24.180sec

Lucy Ogechukwu Ejike (Ngr) – Powerlifting women's-48kg: 130kg

Fatima Omar (Egy) – Powerlifting women's -56kg: 141.5kg

Takayuki Suzuki (Jpn) – Men's swimming 50m breaststroke SB3: 48.49sec

Jessica Long (USA) – Women's swimming 200m individual medley SM8: 2min 42.56sec; Women's swimming 200m individual medley SM8: 2min 41.85sec; Women's swimming 400m freestyle S8: 4min 47.45sec; Women's swimming 100m freestyle S8: 1min 06.81sec

Matt Skelhon (GBR) – Mixed shooting R3-10m air rifle prone SH1: 600pts

Wenbo Wang (Chn) – Men's athletics discus throw F35/36: 38.98m

David Roberts (GBR) – Men's swimming

400m freestyle S7: 4min 52.35sec

Suk-Man Hong (Kor) – Men's athletics 400m T53: 47.670sec

Sergei Punko (Blr) – Men's swimming 400m freestyle S12: 4min 08.64sec

Rik Pendleton (Aus) – Men's swimming 200m Individual medley SM10: 2min 12.78sec

Aldona Grigaliuniene (Lit) – Women's athletics shot put F37/38: 12.58m

Na Mi (Chn) – Women's athletics shot put F37/38: 11.58m; Women's athletics discus throw F37/38: 33.67m

Joze Flere (Slo) – Men's athletics discus throw F32/51: 10.99m

Mourad Idoudi (Tun) – Men's athletics discus throw F32/51: 19.72m; Men's athletics club throw F32/51: 35.77m

Yuan Tang, Yuanrun Yang, Junquan He & Jianping Du (Chn) – Men's swimming 4x50m free 20pts: 2min 18.15sec

Jeremy Campbell (USA) – Men's pentathlon P44: 4662pts

Sherif Othman (Egy) – Powerlifting men's -56kg: 202.5kg

Sam Hynd (GBR) – Men's swimming 400m freestyle S8: 4min 26.25sec; Men's swimming 400m freestyle S8: 4min 26.46sec

Jeff Fabry (USA) – Men's archery individual compound W1: 113pts

Qing Xie (Chn) – Women's swimming 100m freestyle S11: 1min 08.96sec; Women's swimming 100m freestyle S11: 1min 10.36sec

Kirsten Bruhn (Ger) – Women's swimming 100m breaststroke SB5: 1min 36.30sec

Alla Malchyk (Ukr) – Women's athletics shot put F35/36: 9.33m

Evan O'Hanlon (Aus) – Men's athletics 100m T38: 10.960sec; Men's athletics 200m T38: 21.980sec

Oleksii Fedyna (Ukr) – Men's swimming 200m individual medley SM13: 2min 16.32sec; Men's swimming 200m individual medley SM13: 2min 13.84sec; Men's swimming 100m breaststroke SB13: 1min 04.63sec; Men's swimming 50m freestyle S13: 23.75sec

Markku Niinimaki (Fin) – Men's athletics javelin throw F53/54: 29.33m; Men's athletics shot put F53/54: 9.92m

Abdolreza Jokar (Irn) – Men's athletics javelin throw F53/54: 22.08m

Duan Li (Chn) – Men's athletics triple jump F11: 13.71m

Sea-Kyun Park (Kor) – Mixed shooting P4-50m free pistol SH1: 552pts; Mixed shooting P4-50m free pistol SH1: 644.9pts

Oxana Savchenko (Rus) – Women's swimming 100m freestyle S12: 59.47; Women's swimming 50m freestyle S12: 27.07sec; Women's swimming 50m freestyle S12: 27.92sec

Ricardo Ten (Spa) – Men's swimming 100m breaststroke SB4: 1min 36.61sec

Lisha Huang (Chn) – Women's athletics

World records set at the 2008 Paralympic Games (continued)

100m T53: 16.220sec; Women's athletics 200m T53: 29.170sec

Chelsey Gotell (Can) – Women's swimming 200m individual medley SM13: 2min 28.15sec; Women's swimming 100m backstroke S13: 1min 09.09sec

Kamel Kardjena (Alg) – Men's athletics shot put F33/34/52: 11.54m

Jesus Collado (Spa) – Men's swimming 400m freestyle S9: 4min 17.02sec

Mingjie Gao (Chn) – Men's athletics javelin throw F42/44: 57.60m

Hilton Langenhoven (RSA) – Men's pentathlon P12: 3403pts

Bozun Yang (Chn) – Men's swimming 100m backstroke S11: 1min 07.74sec; Men's swimming 100m backstroke S11: 1min 08.40sec

Alexander Nevolin-Svetov (Rus) – Men's swimming 100m backstroke S12: 59.37sec; Men's swimming 100m backstroke S12: 1min 00.78sec

Qing Xu (Chn) – Men's swimming 50m butterfly S6: 31.89sec; Men's swimming 50m freestyle S6: 29.78sec

Olena Akopyan (Ukr) – Women's swimming 50m butterfly S6: 40.51sec

Jason Smyth (Ire) – Men's athletics 100m T13: 10.620sec; Men's athletics 100m T13: 10.810sec; Men's athletics 200m T13: 21.430sec; Men's athletics 200m T13: 21.810sec

Rong Tian (Chn) – Men's swimming 50m butterfly S7: 30.09sec; Men's swimming 50m butterfly S7: 30.37sec

Min Huang (Chn) – Women's swimming 50m butterfly S7: 34.60sec; Women's swimming 50m butterfly S7: 34.47sec

Jarrett Perry (USA) – Men's swimming 100m backstroke S9: 1min 03.47sec

Justin Zook (USA) – Men's swimming 100m backstroke S10: 1min 01.15sec

Shireen Sapiro (RSA) – Women's swimming 100m backstroke S10: 1min 10.57sec

Sophie Pascoe (NZL) – Women's swimming 100m backstroke S10: 1min 10.57sec

Pin Xiu Yip (Sin) – Women's swimming 50m freestyle S3: 57.04sec; Women's swimming 50m backstroke S3: 57.92sec

Weihai Zheng (Chn) – Men's athletics discus throw F57/58: 49.09m

Fuying Jiang (Chn) – Women's swimming 50m butterfly S6: 38.44sec

Sen Yang (Chn) – Men's athletics 100m T35: 12.290sec

Stephanie Dixon (Can) – Women's swimming 100m backstroke S9: 1min 09.30sec

Perla Bustamante (Mex) – Women's athletics 100m T42: 16.320sec

Jimisu Menggen (Chn) – Women's athletics discus throw F40: 28.04m

Antonia Balek (Cro) – Women's athletics javelin throw F33/52/53: 12.82m; Women's athletics shot put F32-34/52/53: 5.69m

Louadjeda Benoumessad (Alg) – Women's athletics javelin throw F33/34/52/53: 17.28m

Jiaxin Bian (Chn) – Powerlifting women's -60kg: 135kg

Taoying Fu (Chn) – Powerlifting women's -67.50kg: 145.5kg

Maria Poiani Panigati (Ita) – Women's swimming 50m freestyle: 31.21sec

Xiaofu Wang (Chn) – Men's swimming 50m freestyle S8: 26.83sec; Men's swimming 50m freestyle S8: 26.45sec

Oksana Zubkovska (Ukr) – Women's athletics long jump F12: 6.28m

Rebecca Chin (GBR) – Women's athletics discus throw F37/38: 33.58m

Chantal Petitclerc (Can) – Women's athletics 200m T54: 27.520sec; Women's athletics 200m T54: 28.250sec; Women's athletics 800m T54: 1min 45.190sec

Liang Fan (Chn) – Men's athletics discus throw F53/54: 31.08m

Zhao Ji, Li Huzaho, Zhang Lixin & Zong Kai (Chn) – Men's athletics 4x400m relay T53/T54: 3min 05.670sec; Men's athletics 4x400m relay T53/T54: 3min 08.800sec

Cameron Leslie (NZL) – Men's swimming 150m individual medley SM4: 2min 33.57sec

Karina Lauridsen (Den) – Women's swimming 150m individual medley SM4: 2min 47.84sec

Eleanor Simmonds (GBR) – Women's swimming 400m freestyle S6: 5min 41.34sec

Tomoya Ito (Jpn) – Men's athletics 800m T52: 1min 52.310sec

Mykola Zhabnyak (Ukr) – Men's athletics discus throw F37/38: 52m

Hania Aidi (Tun) – Women's athletics javelin throw F54-56: 16.83m

Heba Said Ahmed (Egy) – Powerlifting women's -82.50kg: 155kg

Ganna Ielisavetska (Ukr) – Women's swimming 50m backstroke S2: 1min 13.64sec

Sara Carracelas (Spa) – Women's swimming 50m backstroke S2: 1min 18.31sec; Women's swimming 50m backstroke S2: 1min 16.33sec

Byeong-Eon Min (Kor) – Men's swimming 50m backstroke S3: 45.85sec

Faouzi Rzig (Tun) – Men's athletics javelin throw F33/34/52: 34.81sec

Yue Yang (Chn) – Women's athletics discus throw F42-46: 42.38m; Women's athletics discus throw F42-46: 36.99m

Paschalis Stathelakos (Gre) – Men's athletics shot put F40: 11.75m

Leo-Pekka Tahti (Fin) – Men's athletics 100m T54: 13.760sec

Yanhong, Hongzhi Fu, Fangxia Gao (Chn) – Women's archery team recurve Open: 205pts

Marcin Awizen (Pol) – Men's athletics 800m T46: 1min 52.360sec

Wa Wai So (HKG) – Men's athletics 200m T36: 24.650sec

Hongzhuan Zhou (Chn) – Women's athletics 800m T53: 1min 57.250sec

Michelle Stilwell (Can) – Women's athletics 100m T52: 19.970sec

Nely Miranda (Mex) – Women's swimming 50m freestyle S4: 46.27sec

Raoua Tlili (Tun) – Women's athletics shot put F40: 8.95m

Mirjam de Koning-Peper (Ned) – Women's swimming 50m freestyle S6: 35.60sec

Huzhao Li (Chn) – Men's athletics 800m T53: 1min 36.30sec

Ben Austin, Matthew Cowdrey, Peter Leek & Rick Pendleton (Aus) – Men's swimming 4x100m medley relay 34pts: 4min 11.90sec

Olokhan Musayev (Aze) – Men's athletics shot put F55/56: 13.49m

Liu Xiangkun, Li Qiang, Yang Yuging & Li Yansong (Chn) – Men's athletics 4x100m relay T11-T13: 42.75sec; Men's athletics 4x100m relay T11-T13: 42.80sec

Yuan Tang, Yuanrun Yang, Jianping Du & Qing Xu (Chn) – Men's swimming 4x50m medley relay 20pts: 2min 33.15sec

Jim Bob Bizzell, Brian Frasure, Casey Tibbs & Jerome Singleton (USA) – Men's athletics 4x100m relay T42-T46: 42.750sec

Wojtek Czyz (Ger) – Men's athletics long jump F42/44: 6.50m

Artem Arefyev (Rus) – Men's athletics 800m T36: 2min 08.830sec

Mauro Maximo (Mex) – Men's athletics shot put F53/54: 8.72m

Mohammadreza Mirzaei Jaberi (Irn) – Men's athletics javelin throw F57/58: 40.84m

Fanie van der Merwe (RSA) – Men's athletics 200m T37: 23.840sec

Fang Wang (Chn) – Women's athletics 100m T36: 13.820sec

Sanaa Benhama (Mor) – Women's athletics 100m T13: 12.280sec

Evan O'Hanlon, Darren Thrup, Christopher Mullins & Tim Sullivan (Aus) – Men's athletics 4x100m relay T35-T38: 44.810sec

Ting Zhang, Hongjiao Dong, Wenjun Liu & Lisha Huang (Chn) – Women's athletics 4x100m T53/T54: 57.610sec

Jim Bob Bizzell (USA) – Men's athletics 400m T44: 50.980sec

Oscar Pistorius (RSA) – Men's athletics 400m T44: 47.490sec

Bond Qi (Chn) – Powerlifting men's -100kg: 247.5kg

Kazem Rajabi Golojeh (Irn) – Powerlifting men's +100kg: 265kg

Thomas Geierspichler (Aut) – Men's marathon T52: 1hr 40min 07.000sec

Shun Qi (Chn) – Men's Marathon T12: 2hr 30min 32.000sec

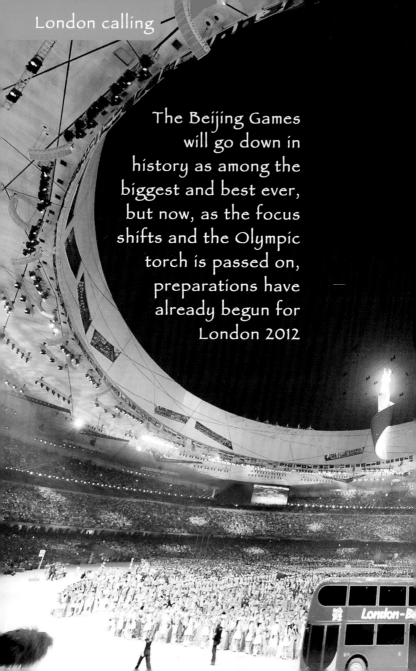

The Beijing Games will go down in history as among the biggest and best ever, but now, as the focus shifts and the Olympic torch is passed on, preparations have already begun for London 2012

London calling

A London bus takes centre stage in the Bird's Nesf as 2012 organisers play their part in the Beijing Olympics closing ceremony

Football superstar
David Beckham
kicks off London's
Olympic build-up
during the Beijing
closing ceremony

London calling

London Mayor Boris Johnson takes custody of the Olympic flag

12 for 2012

Anna Blyth
(Cycling)
Blyth is junior world and European champion. Cycling boss Dave Brailsford would have taken her to Beijing had he been able to pick a second sprinter after Victoria Pendleton.

Olympics Minister Tessa Jowell and Prime Minister Gordon Brown welcome home diver Tom Daley, expected to be one of the stars of the London Olympics in 2012

London be different, and what has the capital learned from Beijing as the countdown begins?

Well, for a start, the organisers will have taken away from China a better understanding of just how important the atmosphere of the Games is.

It is likely that London's Olympic Park will be the focus of public attention in 2012. The suggestion is that a ticketed ground pass system, similar to the tennis at Wimbledon, will allow visitors to pay a small sum to get inside the park, sample the atmosphere and watch events on big screens, even if they do not hold tickets for the venues themselves. Think 'Henman Hill' comes to the Olympics, and organisers have already identified a riverside location with a giant screen on the opposite bank, where visitors will be able to picnic and watch the action. It's all part of the effort to get the whole country involved.

'We have learned the importance of extending access to the widest number possible,' Jowell added. 'This will be UK 2012, not just London 2012, I'm determined about that.'

The idea is to replicate the spirit seen in Germany during the 2006 football World Cup, when fan zones across the country turned the tournament into one big national sporting party. The same

12 for 2012

Aaron Cook
(Taekwondo)
Cook was the first Briton to become a world junior champion in the sport. He missed out on a potential medal in Beijing after two dubious judging decisions.

London calling

An artist's impression of how the London Olympic Stadium will look

12 for 2012

Tom Daley
(Diving)

The 14-year-old diving sensation has targeted gold at London 2012 since breaking into the senior ranks. He was British Under-18 champion at the age of only 12.

approach will be taken in the United Kingdom, and in the years leading up to 2012 the biggest project of erecting big screens at numerous venues around the country will be announced.

If organisers get the atmosphere right, then the Games will be an undoubted success. That is why Sydney in 2000 is viewed as one of the best Games ever: the whole of Australia got on board for those two weeks and made it an unforgettable experience. Beijing showed just what is possible on that score too. There were more than a million Chinese volunteers lending a hand. There will be fewer in London, of course, but there are plans to recruit volunteers from a wide range of ages – as was the case in the Manchester Commonwealth Games in 2002 – and that should help to make the experience just as unforgettable for those visiting from overseas as it will be for the hosts.

Transportation is a key issue for any

Prime Minister Gordon Brown and London Mayor Boris Johnson are shown a model of the Olympic Stadium by Olympic Delivery Authority chairman John Armitt

12 for 2012

Luol Deng
(Basketball)
Born in Sudan but raised in London, Deng is an NBA star with the Chicago Bulls and would be Great Britain's equivalent to Chinese superstar Yao Ming.

Games and with a massive influx of people to cater for, London's planners insist they will pull out all the stops to ensure athletes and spectators get to the right place, at the right time, with the minimum of fuss.

'London is a world-class city and deserves world-class transport,' said the city's Mayor, Boris Johnson. 'The 2012 Olympic Games gives us a deadline to deliver the necessary changes, on top of what we are already achieving, and

Building work in progress on the Olympic Park site in east London

12 for 2012

Paul Drinkhall
(Table tennis)
Drinkhall is Britain's number one, but his aim is to be the Roger Federer of table tennis and top the world rankings by 2012.

12 for 2012

Jason Kenny
(Cycling)
Kenny was tipped for 2012 success when he won the world junior equivalent to Chris Hoy's medal hat-trick in 2006. He is ahead of schedule, having won gold and silver in Beijing.

the Paralympic Games will help us focus on making the network more accessible for those who find travelling in the capital difficult.'

With a total budget for the entire Games in the region of £9.3billion, it looks certain a large chunk of money will be allocated to ensure the city lives up to its promise.

And that is to say nothing of the planned Olympic Village, which, according to Johnson, will cater to the athletes' every need and allow them to perform to their maximum.

'They are going to have a fantastic Olympic Village in which to spend their time during the Games,' Johnson added. 'In the long term, those 3,000 units we are building in east London are going to be a vital part of the legacy we want to see out of the Olympic Games.'

Putting the athletes first is at the heart of what London's Games will stand for, and Lord Sebastian Coe, chairman of the 2012 organising committee, admits his mantra has hardly changed since the day he took over as head of the bid back in 2004.

He said: 'If anything, my commitment has strengthened after visiting Beijing this summer. Put simply, there are no Games without the athletes, no breathtaking moments of sporting brilliance, no spine-tingling magic that lives in the memory long after the Games are over.'

Coe is right, a great Games needs to have those spine-tingling moments. In Beijing it was Usain Bolt demolishing three sprinting world records, and Michael Phelps breaking Mark Spitz's landmark to win eight gold medals in the pool. In Sydney it was Cathy Freeman coming home in the 400m, and Steve Redgrave's fifth successive gold in the rowing.

London will no doubt have its own golden memories, and hopefully its own home heroes to catch the public imagination.

The final lesson that London will have learned from Beijing is perhaps the most important one. For the Games to be truly judged a success there need to be plenty of British medals for the crowds to cheer. The host nation's athletes can inspire the whole country, as China's feats of excellence in Beijing proved.

Britain's 19 gold medals, and 47 in all, at the 2008 Games – their best Olympic performance in 100 years – was a staggering achievement, and Team GB will seek to go even better in four years' time.

Fortunately, the money is being spent to ensure that is the case, to the tune of £100million a year from public funds going into Olympic sport via funding

12 for 2012

Shanaze Reade
(Cycling)
Young, articulate and fiercely competitive, Reade should be the face of the London Olympics. Already a BMX star having just missed a medal in Beijing, she is likely to be a track racer by 2012.

12 for 2012

Greg Rutherford
(Athletics)
Rutherford will be determined to
win long jump gold in London
after leaving the Games in Beijing
furious at having blown a medal
chance in what was a relatively
weak field.

12 for 2012

Louis Smith
(Gymnastics)
Smith won Britain's first gymnastics medal since 1908 when he claimed bronze on the pommel horse in China. He is also Commonwealth champion and world bronze medallist.

12 for 2012

Stephanie Twell
(Athletics)
Twell is the world cross-country champion at junior level, and is rated as Britain's best distance running prospect since Paula Radcliffe.

body UK Sport. It has been proved in the past that spending cash in the right way – on the best coaches, experts and facilities – is a sure-fire way of achieving success. The challenge for London is to translate that into improving wider participation in sport.

Coe added: 'I've always felt the primary purpose of a medal is that it signifies a big British moment. And big British moments in sport have to have a conversion rate. For the Chris Hoys of this world, and our rowers and swimmers, the real challenge for our governing bodies and for sport more broadly is, how many people can you get into the sport off the back of that great moment?

'I'm a football fan, and we have to accept that it's our national sport, but I do think we can really elevate the status of some of our Olympic sports. We want fewer couch potatoes and more participants, but I also want full stadia.'

That could be the real legacy of the 2012 Olympics. When the Games are gone, London, and British sport as a whole, should have a platform from which to build for the future. The organisers are confident that will prove to be the case and that the city will deliver a spectacular showpiece.

'We will draw on our heritage and we will draw on our wit, flair,

London's Olympic flag flutters in the Mall in readiness for 2012

imagination and ingenuity,' added Johnson. 'We will build on what we've all witnessed in Beijing and deliver a fantabulous Olympics in what I consider to be not only my home, but the home of sport. Sport is coming home. See you in London!'

12 for 2012

Khalid Yafai
(Boxing)
The former world junior flyweight champion vowed to fight on as an amateur until 2012 after losing to top-class Cuban Andry Laffita in Beijing.

If you want to get involved in an Olympic sport, here's how to get in touch:

ARCHERY
The Grand National Archery Society
Lilleshall National Sports Centre,
nr Newport, Shropshire, TF10 9AT
Tel: 01952 677 888
Web: www.gnas.org

ATHLETICS
UK Athletics, Athletics House, Central
Boulevard, Blythe Valley Park, Solihull,
West Midlands, B90 8AJ
Tel: 0121 713 8400
Web: www.ukathletics.net

BADMINTON
Badminton England, National Badminton
Centre, Milton Keynes, MK8 9LA
Tel: 01908 268 400
Web: www.badmintonengland.co.uk

BASEBALL
British Baseball Federation, c/o
BaseballSoftballUK, Ariel House, 74a
Charlotte Street, London, W1T 4QJ
Tel: 020 7453 7055
Web: www.britishbaseball.org

BASKETBALL
British Basketball Federation, PO Box
3971, Sheffield, S9 3TW
Tel: 0131 539 9666
Web: www.british-basketball.co.uk

BEACH VOLLEYBALL
See Volleyball

BOXING
Amateur Boxing Association of England,
EIS Sheffield, Coleridge Road, Sheffield,
S9 5AD
Tel: 0114 223 5654
Web: www.abae.org.uk

CANOEING
British Canoe Union, 18 Market Place,
Bingham, Notts, NG13 8AP
Tel: 0845 370 9500
Web: www.bcu.org.uk

CYCLING
British Cycling, National Cycling Centre,
Stuart Street, Manchester, M11 4DQ
Tel: 0161 274 2000
Web: www.britishcycling.org.uk

DIVING
See Swimming

EQUESTRIAN
British Equestrian Federation, Stoneleigh,
Kenilworth, Warwickshire, CV8 2RH
Tel: 02476 698 871
Web: www.bef.co.uk /
www.equestrianteamgbr.com

FENCING
British Fencing Association, 1 Baron's
Gate, 33/35 Rothschild Road, London,
W4 5HT
Tel: 020 8742 3032
Web: www.britishfencing.com

FOOTBALL
Football Association, 25 Soho Square,
London, W1D 4FA
Tel: 020 7745 4545
Web: www.thefa.com

GYMNASTICS
British Gymnastics, Ford Hall, Lilleshall
NSC, Newport, Shropshire, TF10 9NE
Tel: 0845 129 7129
Web: www.british-gymnastics.org

HANDBALL
British Handball Association,
40 Newchurch Road, Rawtenstall,
Rosendale, Lancashire, BB4 7QX
Tel: 01706 229 354
Web: www.britishhandball.com

HOCKEY
Great Britain Hockey Ltd, Bisham Abbey
NSC, Nr Marlow, Bucks, SL7 1RT
Tel: 01628 470 630
Web: www.greatbritainhockey.co.uk

JUDO
British Judo Association, Suite B,
Loughborough Technology Park,
Epinal Way, Loughborough,
Leicestershire, LE11 3GE
Tel: 01509 631 670
Web: www.britishjudo.org.uk

MODERN PENTATHLON
Modern Pentathlon Association of GB,
Norwood House, University of Bath,
Claverton Down, Bath, BA2 7AY
Tel: 01225 386 808
Web: www.mpagb.org.uk

ROWING
Amateur Rowing Association, 6 Lower
Mall, London, W6 9DJ
Tel: 0208 237 6700
Web: www.ara-rowing.org

SAILING
Royal Yachting Association, RYA House,
Ensign Way, Hamble, Hants, SO31 4YA
Tel: 02380 604 100
Web: www.rya.org.uk

SHOOTING
British Shooting, Edmonton House, Bisley
Camp, Brookwood, Woking, Surrey,
GU24 0NP
Tel: 01483 486 948
Web: www.britishshooting.org.uk

SOFTBALL
See Baseball

SWIMMING
British Swimming, Harold Fern House,
Derby Square, Loughborough,
Leicestershire, LE11 0AL
Tel: 01509 618 700
Web: www.britishswimming.org

SYNCHRONISED SWIMMING
See Swimming

TABLE TENNIS
British Table Tennis Federation Ltd, Alex
Murdoch, Harwood House, 90
Broadway, Letchworth, Herts, SG6 3PH
Tel: 01462 671 191

TAEKWONDO
British Taekwondo Control Board (WTF),
Manchester Tennis Centre, Sportcity
Way, Sportcity, Manchester, M11 3FF
Tel: 0161 223 7071
Web: www.britishtaekwondo.org.uk

TENNIS
Lawn Tennis Association, The National
Tennis Centre, 100 Priory Lane,
Roehampton, London, SW15 5JQ
Tel: 020 8487 7000
Web: www.lta.org.uk

TRAMPOLINE
See Gymnastics

TRIATHLON
British Triathlon Federation, PO Box 25,
Loughborough, LE11 3WX
Tel 01509 226 161
Web: www.britishtriathlon.org

VOLLEYBALL
British Volleyball Federation, Suite B,
Loughborough Technology Park, Epinal
Way, Loughborough, Leics, LE11 3GE
Tel: 01509 631 699
Web: www.volleyballengland.org

WATER POLO
See Swimming

WEIGHTLIFTING
British Amateur Weightlifting Association,
Lilleshall National Sports Centre, Nr
Newport, Shropshire, TF10 9AT
Tel: 01952 604 201
Web: www.bwla.co.uk

WRESTLING
British Amateur Wrestling Association,
41 Great Clowes Street, Salford,
Manchester, M7 9RQ
Tel: 0161 832 9209
Web: www.britishwrestling.org